The *Remembered* Woman

A Soul Conversation for the
One Who's Remembering

By
Kalee Boisvert

© 2025 Kalee Boisvert

All rights reserved. No part of this publication may be reproduced, distributed, or transmitted in any form or by any means, including photocopying, recording, or other electronic or mechanical methods, without the prior written permission of the publisher, except in the case of brief quotations embodied in critical reviews and certain other non-commercial uses permitted by copyright law.

For permission requests, please contact:

rememberedwoman@gmail.com

DEDICATION

*To the woman who is just beginning to remember—
May these pages hold you. Speak to you. Remind you.
You are not broken. You are becoming.
And to my children, who inspire the
remembering in me every day.*

CONTENTS

Note to the Reader	1
What It Means to Remember	3
Before the Days: A Soul Orientation	5
Day One: This Is Where the Remembering Begins	9
Day Two: The Day You Turned Toward Yourself	15
Day Three: You Kept Thinking It Was Outside You	21
Day Four: The Day You Honored Your No	27
Day Five: Coming Home to Her Body	33
Day Six: Letting Joy In	39
Day Seven: Your Joy is Sacred, Too	45
Day Eight: When the Strong One Gets Tired	51
Day Nine: You Are Allowed to Rest Here	57
Day Ten: You're Not Behind	63
Day Eleven: Finding the Courage to Speak	69
Day Twelve: Even When You're Doing it "Right"	75
Day Thirteen: Who Carries You?	81
Day Fourteen: You Don't Have to Fix it	85
Day Fifteen: The Girl Who Felt Too Much	89
Day Sixteen: You're Not a Project	95
Day Seventeen: The Quiet Resentment of "Yes"	101
Day Eighteen: The Day You Cracked	107
Day Nineteen: When They Say, "You've Changed"	111

Day Twenty: You're Allowed to Just Get Through the Day	115
Day Twenty-One: Your Softness Is Not a Flaw	119
Day Twenty-Two: You're Allowed to Still Be Healing	123
Day Twenty-Three: The One Who Needs Support	127
Day Twenty-Four: Wanting More (Even When Life Looks Good)	133
Day Twenty-Five: When Healing Becomes the Hustle	137
Day Twenty-Six: Wanting Something Different Now	141
Day Twenty-Seven: You Don't Have to be the Easy One	145
Day Twenty-Eight: Be a Little Messy	149
Day Twenty-Nine: When the Speed Becomes Too Much	153
Day Thirty: What if This Isn't it?	159
Day Thirty-One: Begin Before You're Ready	163
Day Thirty-Two: The Woman You Used to Be	167
Day Thirty-Three: Using Your Voice Anyway	171
Day Thirty-Four: When Healing Doesn't Feel Linear	175
Day Thirty-Five: Let it Be Easy	179
Day Thirty-Six: The Ache of Letting Go	183
Day Thirty-Seven: The Woman You Were Always Meant to Be	187
A Final Gift: You Will Not Forget	191
Acknowledgements	193
About the Author	195

NOTE TO THE READER

Hi, dear one.
I'm so glad you're here.
You don't need to know what this book is—or why you opened it.
You don't have to be in crisis, or seeking, or perfectly still.
You just have to be honest enough to admit something stirred.
That's enough.
That's more than enough.

This is not a traditional self-help book.
No formulas. No ten-step paths. No "how to fix yourself" blueprints.
Because I don't believe you're broken.
I believe you're remembering.

And I didn't write this book from a mountaintop.
I wrote it from the floor.
From the middle.
From the quiet, messy, radiant process of remembering who I really am.

These words came to me like whispers.
Some from my own heart,
and some from the voice that lives deeper still—
the one that only speaks when we slow down enough to hear.

Each entry begins with a story—mine, maybe yours—
and opens into a voice you may start to recognize as your own: your soul.
That voice is labeled **Soul Speaks**—and it's the remembering rising through you.
Each day ends with a message written directly to you—
the woman returning to herself.

The *Remembered* Woman

The one who almost forgot how sacred she's always been.
That section begins with the words:
To you, remembered woman...
Let them meet you right where you are.

After that, you'll be invited to gently reflect.
You'll be given a journal prompt, a breath, or a small practice
to help you live the remembering—not just read about it.

You can read this book a day at a time, letting each message linger—or you can read it in long, soul-deep stretches.
There's no wrong way to return to yourself. Let your intuition guide how you move through these pages.

I wrote this book as a woman remembering herself—
and I offer it to you in the same spirit.
Because you are a remembered woman.
Whether you feel it yet or not.
Whether you've just begun or are rising from the ashes.
Whether you're whispering your truth or still finding your voice.

This book isn't about fixing yourself.
It's about coming home.

And that's what this is, dear one.
A remembering.

WHAT IT MEANS TO REMEMBER

To remember is not to recall a fact.
It's to rejoin with something ancient inside you—something that was always there, waiting.
To remember is to soften.
To stop performing.
To finally feel the ache beneath all that doing.
To hear the whisper that says,
"There's more to you than this."

To remember is to stop reaching outside yourself for answers.
It's the moment you realize:
You were never missing.
You were only taught to forget.

Remembering isn't an epiphany.
It's a slow return.
An exhale you didn't know you were holding.
It's crying at a song you've never heard before—
because your soul already knew the tune.

To remember is to come home.
To come back into alignment with your truth—
not the one the world expected you to wear,
but the one that fits your body like it was made for you.

You were never too late.
You were never too much.
You were never broken.
You were just waiting to remember who you are.

Why This Book is Broken Down to Thirty-Seven Days

There's nothing particularly magical about the number 37—
except that it arrived.
It wasn't forced.
It wasn't chosen for symmetry, numerology, or algorithm-friendly packaging.
It simply showed up as the last thread in the braid.

Because remembering doesn't follow clean timelines.
It's not 30 days to a new you,
or 40 days to transformation.

It's the quiet returning.
The slow unfolding.
The sacred pause between one step and the next.

These 37 pieces came as they needed to—
not all at once, but one by one.
The same way memory returns
when you're safe enough to receive it.

So why 37?
Because that's when the voice said,
"That's enough for now."
And I trusted her.

Before the Days

A SOUL ORIENTATION

For the woman who's starting to remember but doesn't yet know how to explain it.

There are some truths that live deep in our bones,
even if we don't yet have the words for them.
This section is for the woman who has felt the subtle ache,
the quiet pull—
the knowing that there must be more.

Before you begin your journey through the days,
let's return to the questions your soul has already been asking.

What is Source?

Source is not a being in the sky.
Source *is* the sky.
The sea.
The spark in your chest.
The love beneath it all.

Source is where we began—
not as humans, but as energy, light, awareness, presence.

You can call it God. The Divine. The Universe.
The name doesn't matter.
What matters is the remembering:

You are not separate from it.
You were created from Source.
You are still connected to it.
And when you strip away all the noise—
that's what you return to.

What is a soul contract?

A soul contract is a sacred agreement.
Not made from fear, but from clarity.

Before you came to Earth, your soul chose:

- The lessons it wanted to learn
- The patterns it wanted to heal
- The gifts it wanted to offer
- The people it would meet along the way

Some would come to love you.
Some would come to challenge you.
All would play a part in your remembering.

These contracts are not punishments.
They are not meant to bind you in suffering.
They are invitations—
into healing, into strength, into soul truth.

You don't have to understand them all to honor them.
You are already living them.

Why do we choose to come to Earth?

Because Earth is sacred ground.

It is one of the only places in the cosmos where we come to forget.
Where the veil is thick.
Where we don't remember where we came from... or who we truly are...
until we're ready.

The *Remembered* Woman

And that's part of the design.

Your soul chose this forgetting—
not as punishment, but as possibility.

Because to forget your wholeness...
and then feel it stir again in your bones...
is one of the most powerful ways to truly *know* it.

Your soul came here to:

- Feel the contrast of limitation and freedom
- Learn trust inside the unknown
- Heal old wounds through choice
- Express divine energy through human form
- And most of all—to remember itself inside the forgetting

Earth is not easy.
But it is sacred.
Because it is the one place where you can forget...
and still find your way back.

This was never about becoming.
It was always about remembering—
that you were already her.

What happens when our human form passes?

We return home.

When your time in this body ends, your soul is not lost.
It is not judged.
It is not erased.
It is welcomed back.

You remember everything.
You see the full picture.
You understand why it all mattered.

You meet with guides, loved ones, soul family.
And from that space, you choose again.

The *Remembered* Woman

You might return.
You might rest.
You might support others from beyond the veil.

There is no punishment.
There is no final ending.

Only deepening.
Only love.
Only remembering.

Take what resonates. Leave what doesn't.
Let your own truth rise gently to meet you.

There is nothing you must believe to begin this journey.
There is no doctrine here. No rules. No test.

Only the gentle invitation:
Come home to yourself.
Remember what you already know.
Begin where you are.
Let the days meet you gently.

Day One

THIS IS WHERE THE REMEMBERING BEGINS

I was raised by a hardworking single mom.
I saw firsthand what survival looked like.
I watched her stretch every dollar, every hour, every ounce of herself to keep us going.

And somewhere deep inside me, a belief took root:
That hard work was survival.
That exhaustion was necessary.
That safety had to be earned—and even then, it was never guaranteed.

I carried that belief into adulthood without even questioning it.
It was woven into me.

Work hard.
Stay vigilant.
Don't expect ease.
Be grateful for what you have, and don't ask for more.

I knew it was a belief.
I even named it for what it was: a pattern. A story. A lens.
And I tried to shift it with all the tools I had.

I did the abundance affirmations.
The meditations.
The visualizations.
The mantras.

The *Remembered* Woman

It helped—in moments.
But it didn't reach the root.

Because part of me still believed I had to carry it.
That it was the price of being responsible, grounded, acceptable.
I kept it because it made me feel safe.
Because it made me feel like I fit in.
Because it matched what the world around me said was "realistic."

When you carry a belief that says,
"Work hard. Stay small. Be grateful for survival,"
you're seen as wise.
Humble.
Safe.

But when you start to unlearn that—
when you begin to want more, live softer, trust ease—
it can feel like you're betraying the collective story.

That's why I held onto it.
Even when I was outgrowing it.

And then one day... I reached for it like I always had—
and it didn't fit.

Like putting on an outfit that used to feel familiar,
and suddenly noticing it was too tight,
too small,
too outdated to match who I had become.

It felt almost silly to even try.

That belief—it wasn't me.
Maybe it shaped me.
Maybe it helped me get here.
But it never was me.

And when that truth landed,
everything else began to shift too.

And still—there are days when the pull to forget is strong.
When the distractions feel safer than the stillness.
When the old ways feel easier to cling to than the open space of the unknown.

The world makes it easy to forget.
To scroll past yourself.
To drown in busyness.
To cling to the comfortable stories that once kept you safe.

But you're different now.
You can feel it.
You can't unknow what you know.

That's where the remembering begins.

Soul Speaks

Just because something shaped you
doesn't mean it belongs to you forever.

You are not the belief.
You may have carried it out of loyalty.
Out of survival.
Out of love.

But it isn't who you are.

And now that it no longer fits,
you don't have to shrink to wear it again.

You get to grow beyond it.
You get to stand in a new space—
even if it feels unfamiliar at first.

Let yourself be new.
Let the space feel strange.

You're not lost.
You're remembering.

The *Remembered* Woman

To you, remembered woman...

I don't know if you're feeling it yet.
Maybe it's just a flicker.
Maybe it's heavy and confusing.
Maybe it feels like you're standing between two worlds—
the one you built to survive,
and the one that's quietly calling you home.

I just want you to know:
Whatever you're feeling—
it's real.
It's valid.
And you're not alone in it.

There will be days when the distractions feel easier.
When the noise feels safer than the quiet.
When it feels tempting to slip back into what's familiar,
even if it no longer fits.

That doesn't mean you're failing.
It just means you're human.

And maybe—if you're willing—you could start to wonder:
What if these beliefs—the ones that say you have to hustle for your worth,
or stay small to stay safe,
or expect struggle as normal—
weren't truly yours to begin with?

Maybe they were things you picked up in childhood.
Maybe they were things life taught you later, without your permission.
Maybe you had to believe them once, just to survive.

But if you were a blank slate right now—
if you could create your beliefs from scratch—
what would you choose?

Would you choose to believe you are only as good as what you produce?

The *Remembered* Woman

Would you choose to believe the world is dangerous, and ease can't be trusted?
Would you choose to believe you have to earn love, safety, belonging?

You don't have to answer right away.
You don't have to fix anything today.
Just sit with the questions.

Because even letting yourself ask them—
even opening to the possibility that there's another way—
is part of your remembering.

You're not broken because you feel lost sometimes.
You're not failing because the remembering feels heavy.
You're not too late to come home to yourself.

You are already in it.
Even if it's messy.
Even if it's tender.
Even if you can't name it yet.

And I'll be here beside you, in the remembering.

Reflection

JOURNAL OR MEDITATION

Prompt:

Think about some of the beliefs you've carried—about yourself, about the world.
Where do you think they came from?
Were they taught to you?
Modeled for you?
Picked up just to survive?
If you were a blank slate today,
what would you want to believe instead?
Write it down—not as a task to fix yourself,
but as a way of gently meeting yourself where you are.

Gentle Practice:

Sit somewhere quietly.
Close your eyes.
Place a hand over your heart.
And ask yourself, softly:
"What would it feel like to trust that I am already enough?"
No pressure to force an answer.
Just breathe and listen.

Day Two

THE DAY YOU TURNED TOWARD YOURSELF

I didn't even realize how tense I had been
until I allowed myself a breath of fresh air.

As I stepped out my front door, the wind touched my skin.
It smelled like spring.
Not flowers and perfume—
but earth and warmth and beginning.

I was on a walk.
Not for exercise.
Not to hit my step count—which I rarely do anyway.

I had promised myself a Starbucks.
That was the excuse I gave to get out of the house.
To step away from my laptop—
which easily could've kept me going for hours.

There's always one more thing.
One more message.
One more tab open in my brain.

But that day… I chose something else.
Just to be alone.
Just to feel the sun.

The *Remembered* Woman

Just to move without a deadline or destination
(well, other than to a chai tea latte).

And for a moment—
just a small, stolen one—
I felt something soft rise in me.

It wasn't joy, exactly.
It wasn't pride.
It was more like... a return.

Like my body whispering,
"Thank you for letting me breathe again."

And I realized—maybe that was enough.

There was no breakthrough. No declaration.
Just me, outside, in the smell of spring—
not abandoning myself.

Soul Speaks

You don't need a Hollywood moment to return to yourself.
Sometimes, it's just the quiet choice to pause.
To breathe.
To listen.
To come back to you.

Your healing may begin in the simplest places—
the spaces that look ordinary on the outside,
but feel like a homecoming on the inside.

It might not look impressive.
It might not even make sense to anyone else.

But your soul feels it—
the moment you stop running
and choose to stay.

The *Remembered* Woman

To you, remembered woman...

Maybe you've felt it too.
A moment where you were just with yourself—
no fixing, no forcing.
Just being.

And maybe, if you're honest, it felt unfamiliar at first.
Maybe a part of you wasn't even sure if you could trust it.

You've spent so long carrying the weight of what you were taught:
that you have to be doing, proving, earning your place.
That quiet moments were lazy.
That rest had to be justified.
That being with yourself wasn't enough.

So when you finally paused—
even if just for a few minutes outside, breathing in the air—
it wasn't just a walk.
It was a rebellion.
It was a remembering.

Maybe no one ever told you that it's okay to just be.
Maybe you learned that being still was dangerous, or selfish, or wasteful.
Maybe you survived by staying busy, staying small, staying quiet.

But here you are.
You turned toward yourself.

Even if it felt awkward.
Even if it felt like nothing special.
Even if it scared you a little.

I want you to know: it's okay to feel scared.
It's okay if part of you still doesn't know how to relax into it yet.
It's okay if trusting yourself feels wobbly.

You are safe here.
You are safe in your own breath.

The *Remembered* Woman

You are safe to move slowly.
You are safe to take your time.

Because every time you choose to stay—
to breathe, to notice, to be with yourself without judgment—
you are weaving yourself back home.

You don't have to do it perfectly.
You don't have to even feel ready.
You just have to keep coming back, one small moment at a time.

And every time you do—
your body remembers.
Your soul remembers.

You were always enough.
And you are safe to come home to yourself.

JOURNAL OR MEDITATION

Prompt:

Can you remember a moment—maybe outside, maybe small—when you felt like you belonged to yourself again?
What did it smell like?
What did it feel like in your body?
Write it down like you're painting it back into existence.

Gentle Practice:

Go outside today.
Stand in the elements—whether it be sun, wind, snow, or rain.
Close your eyes.
Whisper:
"I'm here. I'm with me."
Let it be enough.

Day Three

YOU KEPT THINKING IT WAS OUTSIDE YOU

There was a day—
I couldn't tell you the date, only the feeling—
when I realized I was single... and happy.

Not in a defiant, *"I don't need anyone"* kind of way.
Not in a sad, resigned kind of way.
But in a deep, full-bodied, soul-fed kind of way.

And then, almost immediately,
I felt the pressure of the world come crashing in:
"But don't you want someone?"
"Aren't you worried you'll be alone forever?"
"Aren't you missing something?"

And for a moment, I questioned it.
Questioned me.
Wondered if I'd been fooling myself.

Because everyone else seemed so certain
that fulfillment had to look a certain way.

But then I slowed down.
I put my phone down.
I put the stories down.
And I came back to what I actually felt.

The *Remembered* Woman

I wasn't missing anything.
Not in that moment.
I was full.
I was home in myself.

And when I let that truth land, the dam inside me broke.
Years of shame, conditioning, quiet pressure—gone.

All that remained was this:
I was never missing anything.
I was never waiting to be chosen.
I had already chosen myself.

Soul Speaks

You've been taught to search for something outside of you—
to chase, to prove, to wait to be chosen.

But the truth?
You were never missing anything.
You were always right here.

The coming home you're craving
isn't simply in someone else's arms,
or in someone else's approval.

It begins the moment you start choosing yourself.

To you, remembered woman...

Maybe you've felt that tug too—
the one that says you're not allowed to be content on your own.

The one that whispers,
"You should want more. You should need more. You should be chasing something or someone."

And maybe there have been moments where you almost believed it.
Moments where you wondered if something really was missing.

The *Remembered* Woman

Moments where the world's noise got so loud that you questioned your own enoughness.

Because it's not just about wanting connection.
It's the way the world tells you that you have to find it—
that partnership, marriage, and motherhood are the milestones that make you real.
That your life doesn't fully begin until you're chosen.
Until you follow the timeline.

You're told to go on the dates.
To make the profiles.
To stay hopeful and hustling—
because everything seems to revolve around finding someone.

And if you're not chasing it?
If you're not fitting into the plan?
If your dreams look different, or slower, or not traditional at all—
it can feel like you're falling behind.

Maybe you want motherhood someday—
but not the way the world packages it.
Maybe you aren't sure yet.
Or maybe you are sure that it isn't for you.

Maybe your dreams are unfolding differently,
and it's terrifying to trust yourself when the map you were handed doesn't match the one you're drawing.

If you've felt that pressure—
I want you to know:
There's nothing wrong with you.

You are not broken because you don't always feel full.
You are not broken because some days the loneliness feels louder than your knowing.

It's hard to trust your own fullness in a world that profits from your doubt.
It's hard to trust that being home in yourself can be enough.

The *Remembered* Woman

But just for today—
what if you didn't have to explain it?
Or defend it?
Or prove it?

What if your fullness was real—
even if some days it feels fragile?
What if you're not missing anything at all?

It's okay if it feels unfamiliar.
It's okay if you still sometimes wonder.
It's okay to let it be a practice—
not a perfect arrival.

You don't have to perform fullness.
You only have to feel it in small, honest ways.

You are not a project to finish.
You are already whole.

And you are allowed to want what you want—
even if it doesn't look the way you thought it would.
Even if you're still figuring it out.
Even if the world doesn't understand.

You are allowed to feel complete—
no plus one required.

Reflection

JOURNAL OR MEDITATION

Prompt:

Where have you been looking for your worth outside of yourself?
In approval? In achievement? In relationships?
Write down the places you've searched—
and then ask gently:
"What part of me is still waiting to return to me?"

Meditation:

Sit quietly and place a hand on your chest.
Breathe with the phrase:
"I am already home."
Let it echo.
Let it settle.

Day Four

THE DAY YOU HONORED YOUR NO

I was always nice—
a people pleaser to the core.
Accommodating. Easy to love.
The one who always showed up, even when I was already stretched thin.

Then came a request—
a speaking event I normally would've agreed to without thinking.

The kind that looks good on paper.
The kind people say yes to because they're lucky to be asked.
The kind you're *supposed* to say yes to.

The email came while I was away on a trip—Disney with my kiddos.
A magical trip I'd been looking forward to.

And honestly, I probably shouldn't have even been reading emails in that moment.
But I did.
And instead of excitement, I felt it—
that now-familiar tug of depletion.

I didn't feel lucky.
I felt tired.
And not just physically—soul tired.

The *Remembered* Woman

I had been running on empty for weeks,
showing up for everything and everyone but myself.

So when that email came through,
my body gave me the answer before my brain could argue:

No.

And for the first time,
I didn't override it.
I didn't explain it away.
I didn't say yes out of guilt or image or obligation.

I said no.
Clearly. Kindly. Without apology.

And it felt terrifying.
And it felt holy.

Soul Speaks

Somewhere along the way, you were told
that being a good person means being available always.
That love is proven in how much you do.
That being nice means saying yes—
even when everything inside your body is screaming no.

But here's the truth:
You don't need to extend your energy to what others expect you to be.
You don't have to earn rest through a burnout.

And saying no doesn't make you difficult—
it makes you truthful.

A boundary isn't selfish.
It's how you stay loyal to the one who matters most—you.

You can trust that knowing.
And you don't need anyone's permission to protect it.

The *Remembered* Woman

To you, remembered woman...

Maybe you've felt that edge too.
That moment when your body whispered *"no"* while your mouth almost replied *"sure."*

That quiet sting of self-abandonment and disappointment
that followed a yes you didn't mean.

It's okay if it's still hard sometimes.
It's okay if your voice shakes when you honor your no.
It's okay if you feel guilty, or scared, or like you're letting someone down.

Because somewhere along the way,
you were taught that love meant sacrifice.
That being "good" meant being agreeable.
That being chosen meant being available—
even when it cost you parts of yourself.

Maybe no one ever told you that you are allowed to be loyal to yourself first.
Maybe no one ever told you that you can love people and still say no.
That you can be kind and still have boundaries.
That protecting your energy doesn't make you selfish—
it makes you trustworthy with your own life.

If it feels terrifying to choose yourself—
you're not doing it wrong.
You're doing something revolutionary.

Because every time you say no from a place of truth,
you say yes to the woman you're becoming.

And I want you to know:
You're not alone in that.
You're not wrong for finding it hard.
You're not too late to build a life where your peace gets to matter.

The *Remembered* Woman

You are allowed to stay with you.
Even when it's awkward.
Even when it's scary.
Even when no one else understands.

You are allowed to choose you.
Again and again and again.

And every time you do—
you are remembering who you really are.

Reflection

JOURNAL OR MEDITATION

Prompt:

What have you been saying yes to that your soul quietly resists?
Write about one time you honored your no—
or one time you wish you had.
What did that moment feel like in your body?
Now write a sentence you could speak next time—
a clear, kind, unapologetic no.

Gentle Practice:

Place your hand on your belly.
Say aloud:
"I protect my peace. I trust my no. I honor my energy."
Feel it settle into your center.
Feel it strengthen you.

Day Five

COMING HOME TO HER BODY

There was a time when I didn't even see myself in the mirror—
unless I was doing something to myself, armed with the full arsenal of Sephora products.

Pluck.
Pull.
Tame.
Blend.
Conceal.

I wasn't really looking—
I was editing.

Every glance was task-oriented.
Every mirror was an assignment.

There was no space for presence.
No space for softness.

And I remember one morning—
not because I looked particularly different,
but because I actually stopped.

I paused.
I let myself look.

The *Remembered* Woman

Not with critique.
Not with a plan.
Just to see the woman in the reflection—
not the project.

And what I saw wasn't perfect.
It wasn't polished.
But it was me.

A woman who had been carrying me all this time—
even when I was too busy trying to fix her to say thank you.

And in that stillness, I whispered:
"I'm sorry I've been so far away."

Soul Speaks

You don't need an ah-ha moment to return to yourself.
You just need to stop long enough to see what's already there.

You've spent years managing your body.
Measuring her.
Wishing she were just a little different—
a little less here, a little more there.

But here's the truth:
Your body isn't the problem.
She's the safe space you keep forgetting to come back to.

She doesn't want to be sculpted.
She wants to be trusted—held, heard, honored.

Your body has never been your enemy.
She's been asking for peace all along.

The *Remembered* Woman

To you, remembered woman...

Maybe today is the day you stop looking at your body like a project.

But even if you're not ready yet—
even if the mirror still feels heavy—
you are not failing.

Maybe today you just sit with her.
Not to fix.
Not to critique.
Not to squeeze yourself into some old story of worthiness.

Just to notice.
Just to thank her for carrying you through everything you didn't know how to survive.

And if even that feels hard—
if even meeting your own eyes feels like too much—
know this:

It's okay.
It's not weakness.
It's not failure.
It's proof of how tender your remembering really is.

Because for so long, you were taught to edit yourself.
To hide yourself.
To believe your body was something to manage, not something to trust.

And standing here now—
even just breathing here—
is an act of quiet rebellion.

It is daring.
It is brave.

You don't have to love every inch of yourself to belong to yourself.
You don't have to force softness where there's still old shame.
You don't have to pretend it's easy.

The *Remembered* Woman

You just have to come closer.
Even if it's clumsy.
Even if it's one breath at a time.

Because your body was never the enemy.
She was never asking to be improved.
She was asking to be trusted.
Held.
Heard.
Stayed with.

And you are allowed to come home to her—
without needing to be "ready."
Without needing to be perfectly healed.

You are allowed to whisper:
"Thank you for being there for me, even when I couldn't be there for you."

You are allowed to begin again.
As many times as it takes.

Reflection

JOURNAL OR MEDITATION

Prompt:

What's one message your body has tried to send you recently—
that you ignored or overrode?
Write a letter to your body—
not a performance, not a love note. Just truth.
Begin with: *"I'm listening now."*

Body Practice:

Stand in front of a mirror.
Look at one part of your body you usually avoid.
Whisper:
"You're not a project. You're my home."
Let it land.
Let it echo.

Day Six

LETTING JOY IN

I didn't post much about our trip to Hawaii.
It was a dream—a destination I'd kept on my bucket list for years.
And I finally got to go.

With my kids.
With the ocean.
With slow mornings and salty air and memories I'll carry for the rest of my life.

And not just the picture-perfect moments—
but the small, messy, perfect ones too.

Trying a new shaved ice spot every single day with my daughter, Ivy, laughing as we compared flavors and declared which one was "the best yet."

Walking along the beach in the evening after the crowds had disappeared,
when it felt like it was just us and the moon and the sound of our own joy.

Jumping into the rental car without a plan—
setting out on spontaneous adventures,
getting caught in the rain,
spotting turtles in the wild,
and running out of milk for my son, Jax, at the most inconvenient moment.

It was imperfect.
It was full.
It was magic.

And still... when we got home and people asked about it, I noticed something:
I softened the glow.
I gave them the summary version.
I didn't share the moments that made me cry from happiness.

Because somewhere inside me, guilt began to rise:
Not everyone gets this.
Maybe I shouldn't be so openly joyful.
Maybe I should keep it quiet.

So I did.
I tucked the joy away—like it was something private. Maybe even selfish.

And it broke my heart a little.
Because I had finally let myself live something beautiful...
and I was still scared to let myself feel it fully.

Soul Speaks

Somewhere along the way, you were taught that joy is dangerous.
That celebration is unsafe.
That you can't get too high or the fall will be worse.

But here's the truth your soul remembers:
You were not born to be cautiously grateful.
You were born to feel it all.

You don't have to apologize for the light.
You don't have to brace for the crash.

You can let the good land.
You can let it take up space.

The *Remembered* Woman

> And if it fades?
> You'll still be okay.
> You'll survive that too.
>
> But for now—you get to be here.
> You get to feel good.

To you, remembered woman...

Maybe you've been holding your joy at arm's length too.
Just in case.
Just to be safe.
Just so no one thinks you're bragging—
or, worse, so you won't jinx it.

Or maybe it's even deeper than that.
Maybe for a long time, you didn't even let yourself dream of happiness.
Maybe joy felt like a luxury someone else got to have—
something too fancy, too far away, too fragile for you.

Maybe you learned early on that survival was enough to ask for—
and anything more felt greedy.

Maybe you taught yourself not to hope too much.
Not to want too much.
Not to expect too much.

And if you have—
I just want you to know:

There is nothing selfish about your joy.
There is nothing wrong with letting yourself want good things.
There is nothing reckless about being fully alive.

You are not responsible for managing other people's emotions
by dimming your own light.

You don't have to tuck your happiness away
to prove you're humble enough, grateful enough, careful enough.

The *Remembered* Woman

You are allowed to be here.
You are allowed to feel it.
You are allowed to want what once felt too big to name.

You are allowed to let good things happen—
without apology,
without guilt,
without bracing for the crash.

Even if it feels unfamiliar.
Even if your joy is messy, ordinary, imperfect.

You don't have to shrink to be safe.
You don't have to edit your heart to be worthy.

You are allowed to feel good.
You are allowed to stay with it.
You are allowed to let the good land—
all the way in.

No edits.
No disclaimers.
No guilt.

Just joy.
Just you.

Reflection

JOURNAL OR MEDITATION

Prompt:

When was the last time you held back your joy—and why?
What would it look like to let yourself feel good again...
even briefly, even imperfectly?

Practice:

Think of one thing you're proud of—no matter how big or small.
Say it out loud.
Let yourself feel it—fully and without guilt.
Whisper:
"I get to feel good."
Let it echo.
Let it settle.

Day Seven

YOUR JOY IS SACRED, TOO

The more I let myself feel good,
the more I realized just how fragile it felt to share that joy out loud.

Like I had to protect it.
Or worse—justify it.

It was one of those rare days that felt like pure bliss.
Lunch with soul-nourishing women—
the kind that makes you laugh so hard you forget you ever felt heavy.

Then hours at the spa—steam, stillness, warmth, and quiet.
A massage that unraveled tension I hadn't even realized I'd been holding.

And then... the drive home.

I knew what was waiting for me—
a two-year-old bounding toward me:
"Mommy! I missed you soooo much!"

Arms flung wide like I was the sun returning.

It was everything.
It was perfect.

And then came the thought.
The one that pulled me out of my joy and whispered:
"Not everyone gets this."

The *Remembered* Woman

"Some women don't have flexible jobs."
"Some can't afford a spa."
"Your joy isn't fair."

And I felt it—the guilt.
The tightening.
The urge to downplay it all.

But something in me rose up and said:
You don't have to stop glittering just because there is pain in the world.

Because my joy didn't steal from anyone.
And shrinking wouldn't give anything back.

So I let it stay.
The joy.
The light.
The whole thing.

Unapologetic.
Unjustified.
Sacred.

Soul Speaks

Your joy is not a crime.
Your pleasure is not a threat.
Your light does not dim someone else's path.

There is enough grief in the world already.
There is enough weight.

We don't need less joy—
we need more women who feel safe enough to live in full color again.

When you hold your joy, you don't erase someone else's suffering.
But you do model what's possible.

The *Remembered* Woman

So let your joy be safe again.
Let your radiance remind the world what's possible.
Let yourself feel good—without the need to justify it.

To you, remembered woman...

Maybe you've felt that too—
the way joy can sometimes be followed by guilt.

The way happiness can make you feel like you have to explain yourself,
or soften it,
or shrink it,
just in case it's *too much* for someone else.

Maybe you've caught yourself dimming your own light—
turning the colors down—
not because you aren't grateful,
but because you were trying to be careful.
Trying to be humble.
Trying not to take up too much space with your own good.

And if you have—
I want you to know:

You are not wrong for feeling joy.
You are not selfish for holding beauty in your hands.
You are not greedy for letting yourself taste happiness.

You didn't steal your good moments from someone else.
You didn't hoard what was meant to be shared.

Your joy is not an injustice.
Your joy is an offering.

Joy is a color the world needs more of—
bright, unedited, alive.

The *Remembered* Woman

It's not selfish to let yourself shine in it.
It's not wrong to live in full color
when life has room for so much more than gray.

When you allow yourself to stay with it—
to trust it,
to honor it,
to celebrate it—

you remind the world what's possible.
You remind yourself what's possible.

You don't have to downplay the moments that heal you.
You don't have to apologize for the blessings
that came hard-earned or unexpected.

You are allowed to stand in your light.
Fully.
Freely.
Sacredly.

Your joy belongs here.

Not because the world is perfect.
But because it isn't—
and we need women who remember how to feel alive.

Stay.
Stay with your joy.
Stay with your goodness.
Stay with your color.

You are allowed to feel it all.
And you are allowed to let it live.

JOURNAL OR MEDITATION

Prompt:

Have you ever dimmed your joy so it didn't seem "too much" for others?
Write about a moment you wanted to celebrate—but held back.
What would it feel like to let that moment live fully again, guilt-free?

Practice:

Choose one small joyful thing today—and let it be big.
Savor it. Name it. Share it, if you want.
Whisper:
"My joy is sacred. I'm allowed to feel this good."
Let it settle.
Let it live.

Day Eight

WHEN THE STRONG ONE GETS TIRED

There was an exhaustion in my bones I couldn't explain.
It wasn't the kind a nap could touch.
It wasn't something a night off could fix.

It was the kind of tired that lives in your cells—
the kind that builds up quietly,
until you realize your whole body is asking you to stop.

I had just come through a full year.
Building my business.
Releasing two books.
Raising two children as a single mom—
one of whom was still little, deeply attached, and needed me for everything.

I couldn't go anywhere without hearing *"Mommy!"*
I was needed constantly.
Touched constantly.

And I gave and gave and gave…
until there wasn't much of me left to give.

I didn't even realize how depleted I was—
until I felt completely emptied.

And then the new year arrived—
when everyone else felt inspired, refreshed, ready to begin again.

The *Remembered* Woman

I didn't want any of it.
I didn't want a resolution.
I didn't want a fresh start.
I just wanted to be left alone.

It wasn't that I didn't love my life—
I was just carrying too much of it, on too little energy.

And when the exhaustion finally caught up to me,
I didn't think, *I need rest.*
I thought, *What's wrong with me?*

I assumed it was my body's fault.
That I was broken.
That I needed a treatment, or a diagnosis, or a fix.

Because I needed to keep going.
Because I couldn't afford to be tired.
Because there were still people to show up for.

But the truth was—
I didn't need to be fixed.
I needed to be held.

Soul Speaks

You don't have to be strong every moment.
You don't have to smile through it.
You don't have to prove how capable you are to be worthy of rest.

You've done enough.
You've held enough.
You've carried enough.

And now, you get to put some of it down.
Not forever.
Not because you're weak.
But because you are human.

And humans need softness.
Need breath.
Need spaces to be real—not just reliable.

So let yourself be the strong one who also needs a break.
Let yourself be the capable one who also needs to be held.

Let yourself be the one who says:
"I can't do it all today. And I'm still enough."

Let this be your reminder:
Even the strong ones are allowed to rest.

To you, remembered woman...

Maybe that's where you are right now.
Not broken. Just tired.
Not falling apart. Just finally feeling the weight of everything you've been carrying.

And maybe...
you've been carrying it for longer than anyone knows.

Maybe you were the strong one even when you were still just a girl.
The one who didn't want to cause problems.
The one who held things together.
The one who learned how to care for everyone else—
before anyone thought to ask how you were really doing.

You've been the strong one for so long that you forgot what it feels like to pause.
Maybe you're so used to being needed that you've forgotten how to need.

Maybe the thought of resting brings guilt instead of relief—
because somewhere along the way, you learned that rest had to be earned.

The *Remembered* Woman

You've been holding so much.
You've been giving so much.
You've been showing up, pushing through, making it all happen.

And maybe you've done it so well
that no one even noticed how heavy it got.

But I see you.
And I want you to know:

You are allowed to be tired.
You are allowed to not feel okay.
You are allowed to say, *"I can't carry it all today."*

You don't have to wait for a breakdown to justify a pause.
You don't have to explain why you're running on empty.
You don't have to prove anything to be worthy of care.

Even if the world expects you to be the strong one—
you are allowed to be held.
You are allowed to rest.
You are allowed to be human.

Softness does not make you weak.
Needing support doesn't mean you've failed.
Asking for help doesn't make you any less capable—
it just makes you real.

Let this be the moment you stop blaming your body for feeling tired.
Let this be the moment you stop apologizing for your humanity.
Let this be the moment you finally say:
"I need rest. And that doesn't make me less—it makes me honest."

You don't have to keep holding it all alone.
You never did.

JOURNAL OR MEDITATION

Prompt:

What are you tired of holding?
Write a list of everything you've been carrying lately—responsibilities, expectations, emotions.
Then, one by one, write:
"I don't have to carry this alone."

Gentle Practice:

Lie down.
Close your eyes.
Place a pillow over your chest like a grounding weight.
Breathe slowly.
With each exhale, say:
"I release."
Let yourself be held.

Day Nine

YOU ARE ALLOWED TO REST HERE

I was sitting on the couch.
And I wasn't doing anything useful.
No phone. No laptop. No multitasking.
Just... sitting.

And somehow, it felt... wrong.
Like I was wasting time.
Like I should at least be folding the mountain of laundry,
or checking emails,
or making better use of the moment.

Like stillness was wasteful.
Like rest had to be earned.

And my mind immediately offered solutions:
Maybe I should write another book.
Maybe it's time to say yes to a speaking event.
Maybe I should finally bring my podcast back—I only paused it when I had my son.
Maybe I could invest in a business—another income stream, something productive, something useful...

Even in the quiet, the pressure to be "more" found me.
Because I'd been taught that doing meant value.

That movement meant progress.
That rest meant I wasn't trying hard enough.

But I was tired.
And not just "need a nap" tired—soul tired.

And in that still moment on the couch, something deeper spoke.
Not my mind. Not my ego.
My soul.

She said:
"You are allowed to rest—without earning it, explaining it, or feeling guilty for it."

And I exhaled in a way I didn't know I'd been holding.

Soul Speaks

You've been measured by your productivity.
Praised for your strength.
Rewarded for how much you can carry.

But your soul was never a machine, dear one.

You are not more worthy when you're busy.
You are not less lovable when you're still.

Rest is not laziness.
It's not indulgence.
It's not falling behind.

Rest is sacred.
It's necessary.
And it's yours.

You don't have to burn out to deserve a break.
You don't have to fall apart to finally stop.

You are allowed to rest simply because you exist.

The *Remembered* Woman

To you, remembered woman...

Maybe that's exactly what you need today—
not more motivation,
but more permission.

Because you've been told your whole life that your value lives in your output.
That being still is lazy.
That your worth is directly tied to your usefulness.

So when you try to pause—even for a minute—it doesn't feel like peace.
It feels like guilt.
It feels like failure.

Maybe you've felt that voice kick in:
"You could be doing something right now."
"You should be doing more."
"You're falling behind."

And maybe it's gone even deeper—
Maybe you don't even want to rest anymore,
because you're afraid that pausing will only put you further behind.
And that feels unbearable.

So instead of slowing down,
you keep pushing,
keep forcing,
keep numbing—
because you don't know how else to cope.

If that's where you are, I want to say something gently and clearly:

You're not broken.
You're not lazy.
You're not behind.

The *Remembered* Woman

You're tired.
You're overwhelmed.
And you've been carrying the pressure of being "on" for too long.

You were not born for hustle.
You were not made to earn love through achievement.
You do not have to outrun rest to deserve it.

You don't have to write the next book right now.
Or answer the messages.
Or fold the laundry.
Or fix your life in the next hour.

You are allowed to just be.
Without explaining.
Without guilt.
Without productivity to prove your worth.

Stillness doesn't mean you're doing nothing.
It means you're choosing presence over performance.
Peace over proving.
Healing over hustling.

Let this moment be enough.
Let this pause be holy.

Let this quiet be your declaration:
"I am already worthy. Even when I do nothing at all."

You can stop now.
Not because you've finished everything—
but because you are allowed to.

Reflection

JOURNAL OR MEDITATION

Prompt:

When was the last time you allowed yourself rest without guilt?
Write about what rest could look like in your life if it didn't have to be earned.
Where could you soften?
Where could you stop?
Where could you simply be?

Rest Practice:

Today, choose one thing not to do.
Cross it off your to-do list not because it's done,
but because it's not urgent enough to steal your peace.
Then say aloud:
"My worth is not measured by what I produce. I am allowed to rest."
Let that truth settle in your body.
Let it feel like enough.

Day Ten

YOU'RE NOT BEHIND

Not long ago, I had a moment when I looked at where I was and thought:

"I should already have a multimillion-dollar *empire*."
"I should be further along—maybe even on my way to billionaire status."
"I've worked hard, I've shown up, I've built and built and built…"

And then I saw a headline:
Taylor Swift is a billionaire.
And she's younger than me.

And just like that, I spiraled.

But then something in me softened—
because I remembered something deeper than the noise:

Her path and mine were never meant to look the same.
There is no benchmark.
There is no single timeline we're meant to follow.

The idea that we're all supposed to arrive at the same milestones,
by the same age,
in the same order—

It was never real.

I'm not behind.
I'm just walking a path that's mine.
And it's unfolding in divine timing—exactly as it's meant to

Soul Speaks

Dear one, I need you to know something:

You are not behind.
You are not too late.
You are not slow.
You are not less-than because someone else got there faster.

You are simply moving through your life,
at your pace,
with your soul assignments,
on a timeline that honors your becoming.

There is no race here.
No finish line to prove your value.
No spotlight that makes your worth more real.

There's just this moment.
This breath.
This next brave step.

To you, remembered woman...

Maybe you've felt that too—
the ache of wanting to be further ahead.
To already be wildly successful.
To see all your effort turn into something tangible—
not just invisible growth.

And maybe that ache isn't new.
Maybe you've felt it since childhood—
when you were first compared.

The *Remembered* Woman

First measured.
First made to believe that your value came from how well you kept up.
How quickly you caught on.
How impressive you looked next to someone else.

Maybe you were praised when you excelled,
but quietly overlooked when you didn't.
Maybe you learned early on that love felt stronger when you performed well—
when you got it "right."

So it's no wonder that even now,
you sometimes feel behind.

Even when you're doing your best.
Even when you've accomplished more than most people know.
Even when your path has been anything but easy.

If you've ever spiraled into comparison,
or questioned your worth based on someone else's timeline,
I want you to know this:

You are not behind.
You are not late.
You are not failing.
You are not too old.
You are not too slow.
You are not missing your moment.

You are on your own sacred path.
And it is unfolding in the exact rhythm your soul chose—
before you even arrived here.

Your journey was never meant to look like hers.
Or theirs.
Or anyone else's.

You are becoming in your own time.
You are building something real—

even if the world can't see it yet.
Even if it doesn't fit neatly into a headline.

Let go of the timelines you never agreed to.
Let go of the pace someone else set for you.

You don't have to be impressive to be enough.
You're already enough.
Not because of what you've achieved—
but because of who you are becoming in the quiet, unseen spaces.

This is your moment.
Not because it looks like success—
but because you are still showing up.
Still breathing.
Still moving forward in your own way.

You haven't missed anything.
You're right on time.

Reflection

JOURNAL OR MEDITATION

Prompt:

Where in your life do you feel like you've fallen behind—and what timeline are you comparing yourself to?
Whose race are you running?

Now write down:
"What if I'm exactly where I'm meant to be?"
And let your body answer.

Gentle Practice:

Whenever you catch yourself comparing,
place your hand on your chest and whisper:
"My life is not on a timeline. I'm right on time."

Let it land.
Let it soften.
Let it stay.

Day Eleven

FINDING THE COURAGE TO SPEAK

I've lost count of how many times I quieted myself.
Not because I had nothing to say—but because I did.
Because I had something inside me that wanted so badly to be spoken...
and yet, when I tried to share it, my voice came out like a whisper.
Small. Fragile. Like a spark trying to survive a storm.

I remember being in meetings—
sitting around the boardroom table in a career path that was overwhelmingly masculine—
my body holding onto an idea or opinion that I *knew* was valuable.

And I'd build up all the courage I had just to open my mouth.
But by the time the words reached my lips,
my throat would close.
My stomach turned.
The voice that came out didn't even sound like mine.
It was shaky. Timid. Half-apologetic.

And more than once, I thought I might literally be sick from the pressure.

I hated that.
Not because I was weak—but because I *knew* I wasn't meant to stay silent.
I was powerful. I was smart. I was ready to speak.

The *Remembered* Woman

But I had spent so long learning to shrink in order to survive
that even when I finally tried to rise...
my body didn't feel safe enough to let me.

Soul Speaks

Your voice was never meant to stay small.
Your truth was not designed to be watered down.

You are allowed to speak now.
Not just the polished parts.
Not just the sweetened versions.

The honest things.
The hard things.
The holy things.

You can speak and still be loved.
You can be heard without shrinking.
You can take up space without apology.

Let your voice rise because you are remembering.
Let the words come from your soul.

Not everyone will understand.
But the ones meant to walk with you—they will.

And most importantly—you will feel it.
The click. The relief.
Coming home to yourself.

To you, remembered woman...

Maybe you're just starting to feel that rising—
that slow, holy ache in your chest that says:
"I can't keep quiet anymore."

And maybe it's terrifying.
Not because you have nothing to say—

The *Remembered* Woman

but because you've become more and more quiet over time.
Not all at once—but slowly.
Moment by moment.
Year by year.

You learned how to be agreeable.
How to stay soft enough to be liked.
How to translate your truth into something more comfortable for others.

Maybe you were praised for being polite,
for being easy to work with,
for being low-maintenance—
while your real voice sat trembling in your throat.

And now...
even as your truth begins to rise,
your body might still hesitate.
Your stomach might still turn.
Your throat might still close.

That doesn't mean you're weak.
That doesn't mean you're not ready.
It means your voice is sacred.
It means it matters.
It means your body remembers what it cost you to stay quiet—
and it wants to make sure it's safe now.

So let it be slow if it needs to be.
Let it be messy.
Let it be quiet at first.

Even a whisper is a reclamation.
Speak anyway.
Even if your voice shakes.
Even if your words aren't perfect.

The *Remembered* Woman

Because every sentence you say—
in your own words, in your own tone, in your own power—
is a coming home.

You don't have to say it all today.
You don't have to roar.
You just have to begin.

The truth doesn't need to be loud.
It just needs to be **yours**.

Reflection

JOURNAL OR MEDITATION

Prompt:

Where have you been quieting yourself?
When did your voice start to feel unsafe?
What is it longing to say now?
Let it out—unfiltered, even if it trembles.

Voice Practice:

Place your hand on your throat.
Breathe deeply.
Say aloud—even if it's barely a whisper:
"It is safe to speak now. I don't have to be quiet anymore."

Let the sound rise.
Let it be enough.

Day Twelve

EVEN WHEN YOU'RE DOING IT "RIGHT"

Some days, I feel like I'm on a roll.
I'm showing up. Working hard. Loving well.
Trying to be patient.
Trying to stay present.

I'm doing the things we're told matter—
Gratitude. Growth. Gentleness. Grace.

But even on those days…
I might still snap.
I might still feel touched out.
I might still want to run away for a night and not be needed.

Sometimes I lose my patience over something small—
like Jax spilling his snack all over the floor I just cleaned,
or Ivy needing help with a dozen different things all at once,
while a client email dings in
and the 'easy' dinner—just something in the air fryer—burns in the background.

And underneath all of it, there's a cry in me that says:
"What about me?"
What about what I need?
What about the version of me that existed before I became everyone's solution?

The *Remembered* Woman

Because I thought if I just did it right—
if I stayed calm, showed up, stayed soft—
then things would feel peaceful.
Balanced.
Maybe even effortless.

But even then—it's still hard.
And that doesn't mean I'm doing it wrong.
That doesn't mean I'm broken.
That doesn't mean I need to be more grateful, or more spiritual, or more anything.

It just means I'm human.

Soul Speaks

There is no formula that makes life stop being messy.
There is no perfect way to serve others that makes you immune to exhaustion.
There is no version of you who gets it all "right" and never breaks down.

Sometimes the bravest thing you can say is:
"I'm doing my best, but it's a lot."

You're allowed to feel that.
You're allowed to name it.
You're allowed to be whole and weary, all at once.

You don't have to pretend it's all so easy.

To you, remembered woman...

Maybe today, you're not falling apart—
but you're not quite okay either.
You're somewhere in the middle.
Doing your best.

The *Remembered* Woman

Showing up.
And quietly wondering:
"Why does this still feel so heavy?"

Maybe you're carrying the invisible weight of everyone else's needs.
Maybe you're the one holding the household rhythm, the appointments, the snacks, the feelings, the business, the energy.
Maybe you're so good at keeping it together
that no one stops to ask if you're okay.

And maybe—underneath your patience, your gratitude, your grounded presence—
there's a whisper that says:
"What about me?"

Not from selfishness.
From truth.
From a deep longing to feel like more than just the one who holds it all.

And maybe this is the part no one tells you:

You can love your life and still feel tired inside it.
You can feel grateful—and still want a break.
You can adore your people—and still need space from being needed.

That doesn't make you wrong.
That doesn't make you ungrateful.
That makes you real.

You're not broken.
You're not doing it wrong.
You don't need to be more spiritual, more patient, more anything.
You're just human.

And being human is beautiful—
but it's also messy.
Exhausting.
And yes, even the good parts can feel heavy.

The *Remembered* Woman

Let this be your permission to tell the truth—
even if the truth is:
"I love my life... and I'm tired of it today."
Even if the truth is:
"I'm doing everything I can... and it's still a lot."

You are allowed to be whole and weary at the same time.
You are allowed to want softness, space, and a moment that's just for you.

You don't have to earn that pause.
You just have to listen when your soul says:
"And what about me?"

That voice matters.
That voice is you.
And it's allowed to speak.

Reflection

JOURNAL OR MEDITATION

Prompt:

Where have you felt like you're doing everything "right," and it's still not feeling easy?
Write the truth—the stuff underneath the performance.

Gentle Practice:

Place your hand on your chest and say:
"I'm not failing. I'm just human. And it's okay if this still feels hard."

Let the truth be enough.
Let your humanity be holy.

Day Thirteen

WHO CARRIES YOU?

Some nights, I've laid awake at 2 a.m., staring at the ceiling,
feeling like I'm holding up the roof of my family with my bare hands.

The schedules.
The bills.
The emotions.
The bedtime routines.
The school forms.
The car that needs maintenance.
The business that needs attention.
The tiny humans that need me.

I carry so much.
And I carry it with strength.

People say, "I don't know how you do it all."
And I smile.
Because I don't know either.

I joke that it's caffeine. Or chaos. Or my ADHD brain running the show.

But really, it's me—
pushing through, holding it all, staying steady
because I don't know how to *not* be strong.

But sometimes I pause and wonder—
Who carries me?

And I don't ask that with resentment.
I ask it with the weariness of someone who has been so strong, for so long.
And now, my body is whispering:
"Please. Let me rest."

Soul Speaks

Being the strong one can become a kind of identity.
You're the one people lean on.
The one who shows up.
The one who stays steady.
The one who knows how to calm the storm—even while standing in the middle of it.

But dear one...
You don't always have to be the strong one.
You don't have to hold it together while you're unraveling inside.
You don't have to be a safe space for everyone else while denying yourself the same.

Strength is beautiful.
But softness is holy too.
Surrender isn't weakness.
It's the moment you remember—**you matter too.**

To you, remembered woman...

Maybe today, you're close to—or even at—capacity.
You're holding so much.
Balancing it all.
And you're doing it beautifully.
So beautifully that most people don't even see how much it's costing you.

The *Remembered* Woman

You're the strong one.
The steady one.
The one who keeps the roof from caving in—
even when your own bones are tired.
Even when your own heart is stretched thin.

And maybe, like me, you've been that person for so long
that you've forgotten what it feels like to let go.
To say, **"I can't hold this today."**
To let someone—anyone—carry even a little of it for you.

Or maybe there is no one else to carry it.
So you smile.
You joke.
You keep going.
Because you always have.

But I want you to know something you might have forgotten:

You don't have to do it all.
You don't have to be everything.
You don't have to prove how strong you are by never resting.

Even strength needs softness.
Even the safe space needs a safe space.

So if no one else can hold you right now,
then let the ground hold you.
Let your soul hold you.
Let the silence hold you.

You are allowed to set something down.
Even just for a moment.

And no, that doesn't make you any less strong.
It makes you wise.
It makes you real.
It makes you whole.

You matter, too.
And you are worthy of rest.

JOURNAL OR MEDITATION

Prompt:

What are you holding that's too heavy to carry alone?
Write a list of the roles, expectations, and responsibilities that feel like a lot right now.
Then, next to each one, write:
"I can soften here."

Embodiment Practice:

Lie down.
Place your arms at your sides like you're safe enough to release.
Feel the ground hold you.
Whisper:
"I am still strong—even when I allow myself rest."
Let your body believe it.

Day Fourteen

YOU DON'T HAVE TO FIX IT

When my daughter cries, my instinct is to fix it — fast.
Find the reason.
Offer the solution.
Make the pain go away.

It's not because I don't care—
it's because I care so much that it feels unbearable not to know how to help.

And I notice that instinct isn't just in parenting.
It's everywhere in me.

I've always loved math—not just the numbers, but the clarity.
A formula. A process. A promise that if you work the steps, you'll get the answer.
That gave me a kind of peace.
A belief that if I just showed up, followed the steps, and worked hard, there would be an answer.

But life isn't like that.
Life isn't math.
Motherhood isn't math.
Healing isn't math.
Grief isn't math.

The *Remembered* Woman

There isn't always a solution.
There isn't always a next step I can see.
And that part—the not-knowing—can feel terrifying.

But slowly, I'm learning that love doesn't always solve.
Sometimes it simply sits. It stays.

Sometimes, what my daughter needs isn't a fix—it's a witness.
Someone willing to sit beside her sadness, and stay.
Not to rush her out of it. Just to be with her in it.

And maybe… that's what I need too.

Soul Speaks

You are allowed to not know right now.
You are allowed to rest in the mystery.
To pause, even without a plan.
You are allowed to be present without a solution.

This doesn't mean you're lost.
It doesn't mean you're doing it wrong.

It means you're learning a new way—a deeper way—to move through the unknown.
Not control, but trust.
Not fixing, but holding.
Not certainty, but presence.

To you, remembered woman…

Maybe today, you're standing in the middle of something you can't yet solve.
Something open-ended.
Something unanswered.
Something still unfolding.

And maybe it's driving you a little bit crazy—
not because you're impatient,

The *Remembered* Woman

but because you care.
Because you've spent a lifetime being the one who finds the steps,
makes the plan,
holds the map,
solves the problem.

You're not afraid of hard work—
you're afraid of not knowing where it's all going.

You've been taught that love means fixing.
That support means solutions.
That presence means answers.

But I want to offer you something softer, and maybe truer:
You don't have to fix it to be fully present.
You don't have to know what's next to be deeply loving.

Maybe the most powerful thing you can do right now—
for your child, your friend, your partner, your own heart—
is to stay.
To stay near the ache.
To breathe with the discomfort.
To let this moment be unanswered and okay at the same time.

That isn't failure.
That's love in its rawest, bravest form.

You are allowed to pause.
You are allowed to not know.
You are allowed to sit in mystery and still be powerful.

Sometimes the most sacred thing we can do
is just to be here—
without rushing,
without solving,
without leaving ourselves behind.

Reflection

JOURNAL OR MEDITATION

Prompt:

Where are you rushing to fix something—in yourself or someone else—because the uncertainty feels uncomfortable?
What would it feel like to just be with it, instead of solving it?

Gentle Practice:

Place your hand over your heart and say:
**"I don't have to fix this to be present.
I don't have to know what's next."**

Let the words echo.
Let stillness be enough.

Day Fifteen

THE GIRL WHO FELT TOO MUCH

As a little girl, I was called "Kalee Cry Daily."
It was meant to be a joke — maybe even endearing.
But it left a mark.

Because I did cry.
I felt things deeply.
I carried emotions I didn't know how to hold — and the world didn't know how to hold them either.

I was tender.
I was expressive.
I was open-hearted.

But somewhere along the way,
I started to believe that those things were too much.

So I learned to manage myself.
To shrink the feelings.
To push them down.
To be easier.
Quieter.
More agreeable.

Even as I grew up and stepped into bigger roles —
as a mother, a business owner, a speaker —
I felt the pressure to be polished.

Not too emotional. Not too bold. Not too much of anything.
Just pleasant enough.

I tried to stay away from extremes —
too loud, too sensitive, too opinionated.

I knew not to cause offense, or discomfort, or take up too much space.
But in doing so, I became something else:

Watered-down.
Bland.
Neutral.
Not all of me.

And one day, my soul whispered what I had been waiting my whole life to hear:
"You were never too much.
You are allowed to feel it all."

Soul Speaks

Dear one,
Your emotions are not excessive.
Your bigness is not inappropriate.
Your truth is not too loud.

You are not too much —
you are the exact expression your soul came here to be.

You were never meant to be meek.
You were meant to be powerful.
You were never meant to blend in.
You were meant to shine.
You were meant to remember.

The *Remembered* Woman

To you, remembered woman...

Maybe today, you're remembering the colorful parts of yourself that you've muted for too long —
the parts you toned down to be liked,
the parts you edited to feel safe,
the parts you tucked away because someone once told you that big feelings were a burden.

Maybe you were the expressive one, the creative one, the emotional one.
The one who wore her heart on her sleeve.

And somewhere along the way, that light got dimmed.
Not because you weren't worthy —
but because the world didn't know how to hold your brilliance.

So you became more agreeable.
More contained.
More digestible.

You weren't being fake — you were being safe.
You were trying to survive in a world that kept asking you to be less.

But here's what your soul already knows:
You were never too much.
You were never too loud, too sensitive, too opinionated, too anything.

You are deep.
You are bold.
You are full-spectrum.

You know how to hold contrast —
to feel the joy and the sorrow.
To laugh loudly and cry freely.
To speak your truth and still be tender.

You are the whole rainbow —
not beige.
Not blendable.

The *Remembered* Woman

Let this be the moment you let the fullness of you return.
Let this be the day you say:
"I will not shrink to make you more comfortable.
I am not too much.
I am me. And that is enough."

JOURNAL OR MEDITATION

Prompt:

Where in your life have you been softening, diluting, or editing yourself to avoid being "too much"?
Write about the version of you who knows how to hold contrast, depth, power, and tenderness — all at once.

Gentle Practice:

Stand tall.
Take up space.
Breathe deeply and say aloud:
"I am not too much.
This is me.
And I have finally come home to myself.
I am remembering."

Day Sixteen

YOU'RE NOT A PROJECT

I read the books.
Lined my shelves with promises of healing.

The spiritual books.
The trauma guides.
The manifesting manuals.

I booked the coaches.
Took the courses.
Wrote the affirmations.
Did the inner child work.
Pressed play on every guided meditation.

I showed up.
Hard.

I became the star student of self-improvement.
If healing was homework, I handed it in early.
If growth was a course, I was on the honor roll.

And still... I wondered:
Why don't I feel better yet?
Why do I still feel like something's missing?
Why do I still feel like I have to work harder—just to earn the right to feel peaceful?

That's when I realized:
Somewhere along the way, self-development became another form of

perfectionism.
I wasn't healing because I loved myself—
I was healing because I was afraid I wasn't lovable yet.

That truth landed hard.
But somewhere deeper—softer—
my soul whispered:
"You are not a project.
You are a person.
And you are already whole."

Soul Speaks

You don't have to fix yourself before you're allowed to rest.
You don't have to clear every block before you're allowed to be loved.
You don't need to finish some invisible checklist to be worthy of love and belonging.

You are allowed to be in process
and still be deeply worthy.

Growth is beautiful.
Healing is sacred.
But none of it makes you more deserving—
because you were already whole before you began.

You can release the grind.
Let go of the pressure to be a perfect student.

Some days, you're allowed to just be.
Breathe.
Laugh.
Play.
Exist.

That, too, is sacred.

The *Remembered* Woman

To you, remembered woman...

Maybe today, you're exhausted from chasing the next version of yourself.
Tired of overworking your healing.
Tired of constantly trying to "improve."

You've read the books.
Sat in the circles.
Filled the journals.
Recited the mantras.
Said yes to all the right things—
not because you were faking it,
but because you really wanted to be okay.

And maybe, along the way,
you also took in the endless stream of unsolicited advice—
the well-meaning suggestions from strangers and loved ones alike.

"Have you tried meditating more?"
"You should really talk to someone."
"Just think positive."
"Be grateful."
"Let it go."

And you tried.
Not because you agreed—
but because part of you wondered if maybe they were right.
Maybe there was something wrong with you.
Maybe you really weren't enough until you healed all the way.

But here's what your soul wants you to know now:

Healing isn't a race.
It isn't a checklist.
It isn't about becoming perfect.

You were never meant to fix yourself into wholeness.
You were meant to remember you were whole all along.

The *Remembered* Woman

You're allowed to pause your growth and still be worthy.
You're allowed to exist without trying to improve.

Let this be the day you stop performing your progress
and start remembering the truth underneath it all:

You were never broken.
You were always whole.
And you still are.
Even here.
Even now.
Even when it's still messy.
Even when someone else thinks they know better.

You are not a project.
You are a person.
A soul.
A story.
A beautiful, living becoming.

Let yourself breathe.
Not to reset your nervous system.
Not to do it "right."
But because you're allowed to just be.

That, too, is sacred.

JOURNAL OR MEDITATION

Prompt:

Have you ever used healing or self-improvement as a way to prove you're enough?
What would shift if you stopped trying to be the perfect student—and just let yourself be human?

Gentle Practice:

Sit with no task, no book, no lesson.
Just you, breathing.
Place your hand on your heart and whisper:
**"I don't have to fix myself to deserve peace.
I am whole, even here.
Even in the becoming."**

Let it land.
Let it stay.

Day Seventeen

THE QUIET RESENTMENT OF "YES"

There was a time I said yes to everything.
Every invite. Every event.
Even destination weekends with friends that came with a hefty price tag.

Not because I had the space for it—
but because I didn't want to be left out.
I didn't want to lose my place in the circle.
I didn't want to seem like the one who couldn't keep up.

So I said yes.
Even when I was the sole financial provider for my daughter.
Even when I was quietly doing what I could to support my sister through her own challenges.
Even when I knew I didn't truly have the space—emotionally or financially—to say yes.

I was already holding so much.
But I still said yes.
With a smile. With a suitcase.
With a quiet ache inside that said,
"I can't afford this — emotionally or financially."
But I said yes anyway.

Because saying no felt like the riskiest thing I could do.
And I convinced myself that this was just what good friends do — they show up, no matter what.

But what I didn't realize was how deeply I was betraying myself.
How every yes that came from fear, not desire, was planting a seed of resentment.
Not just toward them — but quietly, toward myself.

Because I knew better.
And I still didn't protect myself.

Soul Speaks

You are allowed to say no — not just to protect your energy, but to honor your truth.
Your no doesn't make you difficult. It makes you discerning.
It's not rejection. It's self-respect. It's self-remembrance.

You do not owe anyone access to your time, your presence, your money, your peace.

You are allowed to say no to protect your future peace.
To care for your children.
To honor your values.
To stay in integrity with what matters to you.

You are allowed to say:
"I love you... and this isn't something I can give right now."

That's not selfish — it's sacred.
Because every no spoken from truth opens space for the deeper yes.

Yes to your nervous system.
Yes to your peace.
Yes to your healing.
Yes to the woman you're becoming.

The *Remembered* Woman

To you, remembered woman...

Maybe you're holding a quiet resentment—
not because they keep asking,
but because you've stopped listening to your own no.

And maybe it's hard to admit that.
Because you love them.
Because you want to be seen as dependable.
Because you were taught that showing up—no matter what—is what makes you a good friend, a good sister, a good woman.

So you said yes.
Even when your body was begging for a rest.
Even when your finances were tight.
Even when your soul whispered: **"This isn't yours to carry."**

You didn't say yes because you didn't care—
you said yes because you cared so much
that you forgot to include yourself in the equation.

But here's what I want you to remember:

You are allowed to say no.
Not just to protect your energy—
but to protect your truth.

You don't owe anyone your attendance at the cost of your peace.
You don't have to prove your love.
And you don't have to keep showing up in spaces where your nervous system is quietly screaming.

You are allowed to disappoint others in order to choose yourself.
That is not rejection.
That is return.

So if you've been saying yes to avoid being left behind...
Let this be the moment you remember:

You belong to you.
And that bond is sacred.

Say yes from truth.
Say no from love.
And let both be holy.

JOURNAL OR MEDITATION

Prompt:

Where have you said yes to avoid rejection — even when it cost you peace?
What would it feel like to reclaim your no — not as rejection, but as return?

Gentle Practice:

Write down one moment you wish you had said no.
Then bless it with compassion — not shame.
Place your hand over your heart and whisper:
**"My no is sacred.
And my yes is discerning."**

Let it land.
Let it stay.

Day Eighteen

THE DAY YOU CRACKED

I answered client emails hours after giving birth to my son.
Not because I wanted to.
Not because I was rested or ready.

But because I didn't want anyone to assume I wouldn't be as good at what I do now that I had a new baby.
I wanted to prove I could still handle it.
That nothing had changed.
That I was still on it.

But inside, I was cracked wide open — raw, aching, unraveling.
I had just brought life into the world.
My body was raw.
My heart was stretched.
My nervous system was buzzing.

And still, I felt like I had to show up — not just for my baby, but for the world outside of him.

Somewhere along the way, I learned that falling apart wasn't allowed.
That if I unraveled — even a little — someone would question my strength.
Or my reliability.
Or my worth.

So I smiled.
I replied.
I pushed through.

But deep down, I knew —
I wasn't okay.

Soul Speaks

You are allowed to fall apart.
Allowed to not be okay today.
Allowed to be soft, messy, undone.

You are allowed to cry without a reason.
To cancel the plans.
To sit on the bathroom floor and let the weight of it all leave your body — just for a moment.

You are allowed to stop holding it all.

Falling apart doesn't mean you're failing.
It means you're full.
It means you've been holding so much, for so long, that something in you needs a release.

Let it come.
Let it be messy.
Let it soften you.

You don't need to turn this into wisdom.
You don't need to make it useful.
You don't need to package it as healing.
You don't even need to know why it's there.

You just need to listen.

Because every time you crack open,
you make space — for truth, for healing, for light.

The *Remembered* Woman

To you, remembered woman...

Maybe today, you are cracking a little.
Not all the way — just enough to feel the quiet ache beneath your strength.

Maybe you're tired of pretending everything is okay.
Tired of holding it all with a smile.
Tired of being the one who stays steady,
even when something in you is slowly unraveling.

And maybe you've internalized the idea
that falling apart makes you less —
less dependable,
less professional,
less spiritual,
less worthy.

But what if none of that is true?

What if falling apart isn't weakness — it's wisdom?
What if your body knows when it's full,
when it's stretched,
when it can't hold anymore —
and what if your softness isn't something to hide...
but something sacred to honor?

You don't have to be okay to be held.
You don't have to be composed to be loved.
You don't have to package your pain as growth.
You don't have to make it make sense.

You just get to be here — raw, real, remembering.

Let this be the moment you let yourself be held.
By your breath.
By your body.
By your truth.
By the part of you that whispers:
"Even now, I am worthy."

Reflection

JOURNAL OR MEDITATION

Prompt:

Where have you pushed through instead of falling apart?
What would change if you let the tears come — without needing a reason?

Gentle Practice:

Put one hand on your heart and one on your belly.
Inhale for 4, exhale for 6.
No fixing. No bracing. Just breathing.

Whisper:
"I am still worthy — even when I am undone."

Let it soften something in you.
Let it stay.

Day Nineteen

WHEN THEY SAY, "YOU'VE CHANGED"

You know what used to scare me?
The thought that people who once knew me — friends, family, old versions of my life —
might see this version of me and say,
"That's not her. I don't even recognize this person."

And it would sting.
Because part of me still wanted to be recognizable.
Familiar.
Still wanted to be known.

But what they didn't realize was:
This is me.
Not the masked version.
Not the one I shaped to be digestible. To be easy to love.
Not the version I edited down so I wouldn't take up too much space.

This is the version I used to hide.
The one I protected.
The one I muffled with self-doubt and smoothed out with people-pleasing.

So no — maybe they don't know her.
But that doesn't make her fake.
It means she's finally free to speak.

Soul Speaks

You are not "too different."
You are not "too much."
You're not becoming someone else.
You're remembering who you've always been.

This is not performance.
This is remembrance.

Not everyone will recognize the version of you who stopped shrinking.
But that doesn't mean she isn't real.

Let your truth be louder than their confusion.
Let your alignment be louder than their doubt.
Let your peace be proof.

You don't need to stay small just so others feel comfortable.
You don't need to keep performing the version of you they were most comfortable with.

To you, remembered woman...

If someone looks at you and says,
"You've changed" —
take a breath.
Smile, if it feels good.

Because what they're really saying is:
"You're no longer the version of you that made yourself smaller for me."

And that?
That's not failure.
That's not you losing love.
That's you claiming yourself.

The *Remembered* Woman

Because maybe, for a long time, you wore the version of you that kept the peace.
The version that didn't ask too many questions.
Didn't take up too much space.
Didn't make anyone uncomfortable.

You were praised for being sweet.
Palatable.
Predictable.

And somewhere inside, you began to wonder —
What happens when I stop shrinking?
Will they still love me?
Will they still see me?
Will they even recognize me?

And maybe some of them won't.
Maybe some already don't.

But that doesn't make you fake.
It doesn't make your growth a performance.

It means you're finally letting the real you breathe.
The one you used to hide.
The one you silenced to keep things smooth.
The one who has always been there — quietly waiting to be remembered.

Let her speak now.
Let her be seen.
Let her be misunderstood if that's what it costs.

Because what you're reclaiming isn't just a version of you —
it's the whole, radiant, remembered woman you were always meant to be.

JOURNAL OR MEDITATION

Prompt:

Who are you afraid won't understand the real you?
What would it feel like to let that fear exist… without letting it guide your steps?

Gentle Practice:

Place your hand over your heart.
Speak softly to the part of you that is reemerging — the one who remembers.
Whisper:
**"You are not fake.
You are remembered.
And I'm finally letting you be seen."**

Let her feel your presence.
Let her stay.

Day Twenty

YOU'RE ALLOWED TO JUST GET THROUGH THE DAY

Some days, I feel the pressure to make everything meaningful.
To be present.
To be grateful.
To check off every item on the to-do list.
To create something.
To move something forward.
To make it count.

Even when I'm tired.
Even when I'm stretched thin.
Even when I'm feeling something I can't quite name.

And I know where it comes from—
this inner voice that says:
"If you don't make this moment productive, or beautiful, or transformative... then you're wasting it."

But some days, I'm not here to transform.
I'm here to survive.

To keep the kids fed.
To answer a few emails.
To take a shower... or not.
To keep breathing.

And I used to beat myself up for that.
I'd spiral into shame—
that I wasn't doing enough, achieving enough, growing fast enough.

But now I know—
getting through is not failure.
It's sacred.

Because survival is sacred.
And some days, just getting through is the bravest thing I do.

Soul Speaks

You are allowed to just get through the day.
To not make it beautiful.
To not turn it into a moment.
To just... be here.

There is no divine scoreboard measuring your worth in tasks completed.
There is no spiritual penalty for taking it slow.

Some days are not for breakthroughs.
They are for breathing.
Some days are not for building.
They are for being.
Some days are not for showing up at 100%.
They are for showing up at all.

You are not wasting your life when you rest.
You are not falling behind when you soften.
You are not weak for needing simplicity.

Let yourself live without performing your worth.

The *Remembered* Woman

To you, remembered woman...

If today you are weary—not broken, just tired—
and you don't have it in you to make it poetic or profound...

Let it be simple.
Let it be quiet.
Let it be whatever it is.

Maybe you're showing up to your life with half a battery.
Maybe the most courageous thing you'll do today is continue.

And maybe you're used to giving more—
more energy, more presence, more meaning, more effort.

But some days are not for magic.
Some days are just for making it.
And there is nothing wrong with that.

You don't have to turn this into a breakthrough.
You don't have to find the deeper meaning.
You don't have to optimize your rest or make it inspiring.

You can just exist.
Just breathe.
Just do the next small thing.

That is enough.
You are enough.

You are not here to impress the world with how gracefully you carry the weight.
You are here to live.

And even if today looks like soft clothes and tired eyes and an unfinished to-do list—
you still count.

There is no shame in survival.
There is sacredness in making it through.

Reflection

JOURNAL OR MEDITATION

Prompt:

Where are you expecting too much of yourself today — and why?
What would shift if it was okay to just be… enough?

Gentle Practice:

Choose one thing to take off your to-do list today.
Don't replace it. Just… breathe.
Whisper:
**"It's okay to just get through today.
That is more than enough."**

Let it be true.
Let it stay.

Day Twenty-One

YOUR SOFTNESS IS NOT A FLAW

In the early years of my career, I thought I had to trade in my softness to succeed.
I learned quickly that emotion had no place in the boardroom.
That crying was a liability.
That empathy and intuition were not viewed as strengths — only as distractions.

So I tried to harden.
I filtered myself.
I polished my tone.
I kept my voice steady and my face composed.
I carried grief and pressure behind a smile, believing this was what professionalism looked like.

I even cut my hair — not because I wanted to,
but because I thought it would make me seem more polished.
More efficient. More in control.
More like someone people would take seriously.

And still... the softness would slip through.
There were moments the tears came —
not in chaos, not in collapse — just honest human moments that leaked through the armor.

And I saw the shift in the room.
The quiet discomfort.

The *Remembered* Woman

The way their eyes shifted — how suddenly, my capability felt like it was up for debate.

In those moments, it felt like my softness wasn't just unwelcome — it was seen as a threat to my success.
I feared I had ruined everything.

But now... I see it differently.
Now I know that those moments weren't weakness — they were glimpses of the truest part of me.
The part I will no longer apologize for.

Soul Speaks

Your softness is not a flaw.
It is your genius.
Your gift.
Your truest form of strength.

You do not need to become harder to be respected.
You do not need to lose your empathy to survive.
You do not need to turn cold just because the world sometimes is.

Your softness is not weakness.
It is wisdom.

The way you notice.
The way you feel.
The way you care deeply, even when it's inconvenient.

That is not something to suppress.
That is something to honor.

Because in a world that is loud and sharp and fast,
your tenderness is an act of quiet revolution.

The *Remembered* Woman

To you, remembered woman...

If you've been made to feel too sensitive —
too emotional.
Too tender.
Too much.

That you should "get over it" or "be stronger"...
Let me remind you:

Your softness is not your liability.
It's your compass.

You don't have to build walls to stay safe.
You don't have to numb your empathy to be strong.
You don't have to stop feeling to move forward.

Maybe you've spent years trying to sound steady when your voice trembled.
Trying to keep your eyes dry when tears rose.
Trying to filter your words so they didn't shake the room.

And maybe, like me, you feared that if your tenderness showed —
your capability would be questioned.

But here's the truth your soul already knows:
You don't have to trade in your softness for strength.
You are already both.
You always have been.

Your sensitivity is not a mistake.
It's a sign you're still alive
in a world that keeps trying to desensitize us all.

You don't have to apologize for that.
You don't have to tuck that part of you away anymore.

You just have to remember:
You are soft — and still unshakable.
You are gentle — and still powerful.
You are open — and still wise.

Let this be the day your softness comes home to you.

Reflection

JOURNAL OR MEDITATION

Prompt:

Where have you been hiding your softness to protect yourself? What part of your softness is ready to come out of hiding — even if it still feels risky?

Gentle Practice:

Place your hand on your heart and whisper:
**"My softness is sacred.
I can trust it.
It will not lead me astray."**

Let it be safe to be you.

Day Twenty-Two

YOU'RE ALLOWED TO STILL BE HEALING

I thought I was over it.
I did the work.

Shadow work.
Coaching.
The deep, hard stuff.
Said the hard things out loud.
Released what I could.
Reframed what I couldn't.
Wrote about it.
Cried through it.
Carried on.

Then something small would graze that old wound — and there it was again.

Tight chest.
Throat burning.
Heart heavy.

And I'd spiral — not because of the memory itself,
but because of the shame of still feeling it.

Shouldn't I be past this by now?
Haven't I done enough work?
Why is this still here?

The *Remembered* Woman

I thought healing would be linear.
Predictable.
Clean.

But real healing is messy.
It's nonlinear.
It loops and circles and spirals.
It asks for compassion, not control.

Every time I judged myself for still feeling it,
I didn't tend to the wound — I poked at it.

Soul Speaks

You're allowed to still be healing.
To still feel it.
To not be over it yet.

There is no deadline for your healing.
Some things are not meant to be erased.
Some wounds are not meant to disappear —
they're meant to be integrated, honored, held gently.

Feeling it again doesn't mean you're back at the beginning.
It means you're passing through another layer.
A deeper knowing.
A more honest version of yourself.

You are not broken for revisiting the pain.
You are brave for staying present to it.

There is no shame in still feeling tender.
There is strength in honoring what still needs care — and giving it.

The *Remembered* Woman

To you, remembered woman...

If today you are grieving something you thought you were past—
if an old sadness surprised you,
or a trigger you thought you'd "healed" re-emerged...

You are not failing.
This isn't a setback.
It's remembrance.

You are peeling back layers.
You are softening into truth.
You are learning to hold your heart, not fix it.

You've already done so much work.
That doesn't mean you're done feeling.
It means you're human.
It means you're alive.
It means your heart is honest.

So if the tears come — let them.
If the ache returns — stay with it.
Let yourself feel what's real — without shame.
Without hurrying to heal.
Without trying to be finished.

You are allowed to take your time.
You are allowed to still be healing.

And every time you show up for your pain with presence instead of pressure —
you are becoming more whole.

Reflection

JOURNAL OR MEDITATION

Prompt:

What pain are you still carrying shame for — not because it still hurts, but because you think it shouldn't?
Write to that part of you. Let her know she has time.

Gentle Practice:

Wrap your arms around yourself — like you would a child who's still learning how to feel.
Breathe in gently.
Whisper:
**"I'm still healing —
and that doesn't mean I'm behind.
It means I'm becoming whole."**

Let that land.
Let it stay.

Day Twenty-Three

THE ONE WHO NEEDS SUPPORT

I'm someone who feels a lot.
I'm highly sensitive —
I notice shifts in energy, the tone beneath someone's words,
the quiet things people never say out loud.

And that sensitivity?
It's shaped the way I move through the world.

It's why I can show up so fully in my work —
why I can anticipate what a client needs before they say a word.
It's why I can pack for a trip with my toddler
and somehow be prepared for every curveball —
the extra snacks, the forgotten toy, the what-if scenarios that always show up.

That awareness — that deep inner attunement —
makes me dependable.
Capable.
Grounded.

I lead well because I feel deeply.

But sometimes... even when I've got it all "handled" —
even when I've packed the right bag, given the right answer, held the right space —

The *Remembered* Woman

I still long for someone to ask how I'm doing.
To not always be the one holding.
To be held, too.

I remember a moment when I reached out to my mom about something I was going through.
I didn't have a partner at the time.
And I didn't have anyone in my life who really knew me on that deep level —
the kind where you don't have to explain everything… you just get to be held.

And even though I knew she didn't always have patience for emotional stuff…
I reached out anyway.
Because I needed it.
Because I didn't want to carry it all alone that day.

But she couldn't meet me there.
Not because she didn't care —
but because it just wasn't in her capacity to hold what I needed.

And maybe, if I'm honest, part of me already knew that.
Part of me was doing it too —
speeding through my emotions, trying to shortcut the feeling, rushing toward the solution.

And when she reflected that back to me, it stung.
Because I didn't want someone to solve it.
I wanted someone to sit with me in it.
To stay.
To hold.
To not rush my pain into progress.

Soul Speaks

You are allowed to be the one who needs support.
You are allowed to not be the strong one today.

You are not only valuable when you're holding everyone else.
You are not only lovable when you're keeping it all together.
You are not only worthy when you're pouring into others.

You are allowed to fall apart — and let someone else hold you.
You are allowed to ask for help — and not qualify it with,
"Only if you're not too busy."

You are allowed to receive — not out of weakness,
but as an act of trust.

You do not need to earn your right to be supported.
You are already worthy of being met with care, tenderness, and presence.

Let yourself be supported the way you support everyone else.

To you, remembered woman...

If today you're feeling the weight of always being the one who holds it together —
the one who shows up, holds space, leads with grace...

Let this be your permission to put it down.

You do not have to carry everything alone.
You don't have to be the steady one without ever being steadied.
You don't have to offer care without receiving it.

You've built so much strength.
And maybe somewhere along the way, you learned that needing others made you less strong —
less dependable.

The *Remembered* Woman

Less capable.
Less worthy of admiration.

But, the truth is this:
Your need does not make you weak.
Your longing does not make you dramatic.
Your desire to be held is not a burden — it's human.

You can be soft and strong.
You can be wise and wobbly.
You can be capable and still in need of care.

You've been the safe space for so many.
Now let someone be a safe space for you.

Even if that "someone" is your own arms, wrapped around yourself, whispering:
"I've got you now."

Let someone hold you —
a friend, a memory, a divine presence.
Let your soul exhale.
Let yourself be supported.

Reflection

JOURNAL OR MEDITATION

Prompt:

Where have you quietly needed support, but convinced yourself you should be able to "handle it"?
What might change if you allowed yourself to be held?

Gentle Practice:

Place both hands over your heart and say aloud:
**"I am allowed to need others.
I am worthy of being supported too."**

Let it soften you.
Let it stay.

Day Twenty-Four

WANTING MORE (EVEN WHEN LIFE LOOKS GOOD)

I had literally checked off every box on the five-year vision I created with a business coach.
I built a business focused on supporting women.
I wrote a children's picture book.
Then a non-fiction book to help women build money confidence.
I created a community — with education, events, real connection.
I started a podcast.
I added another beautiful little soul to my family.
I bought a home — and then I built a bigger one.

I had done it.
The dream I mapped out years ago?
It had become my reality.

And I was proud.
I was grateful.
But I was also... afraid.

Because somewhere deep in my body, this quiet thought surfaced:
If I've done it all... does that mean my own unraveling is next?

Like I had hit the ceiling of what I was allowed to experience.
Like I had already tasted more joy, fulfillment, and success than I was

supposed to —
and now the other shoe was going to drop.

I didn't know how to let it just be good.
I didn't know how to live in the "after" without waiting for the fall.

And even more confusing — I didn't know how to name the quiet ache that still lived inside me.

I had everything I said I wanted.
And something in me still whispered:
"There's more."

Not more things.
Not more goals.
More soul.
More truth.
More of me I hadn't met yet.

Soul Speaks

You are allowed to want more —
even when your life looks good on the outside.
Even when it's already better than what you came from.
Even when other people don't understand.

Wanting more doesn't make you ungrateful.
You are not selfish for wanting deeper joy, fuller expression, or a life that feels even more aligned.
You can honor what you have
and still feel called toward what's next.

That desire is not a flaw —
it's a compass.
It's your soul tapping you gently, saying:
"There's more life waiting... don't stop here."

To you, remembered woman...

If you've been quietly asking,
"Why doesn't this feel like enough?" —
let me say this gently:

You are not broken.
You are not ungrateful.
You are not too much.

You are expanding.

You are outgrowing what once felt like the dream —
and that doesn't mean you've failed.
It means you've arrived at one layer of becoming...
and your soul is asking what else you're here to discover.

You are allowed to feel the both/and.
Both joy and curiosity.
Both celebration and restlessness.
Both fulfillment and the tug of something deeper.

This doesn't mean you're chasing more to escape your life.
It means your life has grown so much...
that now your soul wants to stretch, too.

Let yourself be curious about what's next.
Let yourself follow the new longing.
Let yourself want what you want.

Even if you don't know what it looks like yet.
Even if you're scared to want again.
Even if others tell you, "Isn't this enough?"

You are not asking for too much.
You are asking to become more of who you already are.
And that is a holy thing.

JOURNAL OR MEDITATION

Prompt:

Where have you been quieting desire because it doesn't "make sense" to still want something more?
What if that ache is an invitation — not a flaw?

Gentle Practice:

Place your hands on your belly. Breathe into your center.
Whisper:
**"Wanting more doesn't mean I'm ungrateful.
It means I'm ready to grow."**

Day Twenty-Five

WHEN HEALING BECOMES THE HUSTLE

There was a time when healing became my whole identity.
Not just something I did now and then — but something I chased.
I filled my days with the next tool, the next breakthrough, the next spiritual insight.
I consumed it all — podcasts, prompts, visualizations, rituals.

And then, one day, I hit a wall.
Not because I had no more healing left to do —
but because I was tired.

I had absorbed so many teachings, so many practices,
that I would've needed a checklist just to remember how to be a "whole" person.
And even then, there weren't enough hours in the day to do it all right.

It had started to feel like another full-time job.
Another way to fall short.
Another hustle disguised as healing.

And in the middle of all that spiritual effort,
I heard something quiet inside me say:

"I just want to live — and not have to wake up at 5 a.m. to earn it."

I didn't want my healing to feel like a performance.
I didn't want peace to feel like something I had to qualify for.

I didn't want growth to be another checkbox proving I was "doing it right."

I didn't need more insight.
I needed space.

Soul Speaks

You are allowed to be done working on yourself.
You are allowed to stop fixing.
You are allowed to just be here.

You are not a problem to solve.
You are not a blueprint to master.
You are not a self-help project that needs to be completed.

You've done the work.
You've shown up.
You've met yourself in the dark, again and again.

And now?
Now you get to live.
To play.
To rest.
To integrate.

Healing is not meant to become your identity.
It's meant to be a passage — not a personality.
A portal — into wholeness, into joy, into embodiment.

You are allowed to be complete — even with loose ends.
You are allowed to feel free — even with tender parts that haven't fully closed.
You are allowed to stop searching — and start living your life.

The *Remembered* Woman

To you, remembered woman...

If you've been tired from all the inner work —
from always trying to evolve, improve, ascend, heal...
This is your permission slip to stop.

Not because you're giving up.
But because you're ready to live.

Maybe you were taught that healing is a lifelong climb.
That you always need to be working toward "better."
That if something still hurts, it means you haven't done enough yet.

But what if the pain isn't a problem?
What if the ache doesn't mean you're broken?
What if you're not meant to keep digging — but to start rooting?

You are not here to be in constant repair.
You are here to bloom.
To laugh.
To rest.
To build a life that feels like breath, not effort.

You've planted so many seeds.
You've pulled so many weeds.
You've sat with your shadows, your patterns, your past.

Now let yourself rest in the garden you've already planted.
Let yourself notice what's already blooming.

You don't need to earn your worthiness.
You already belong to yourself.
You're already whole.

Let your life begin again —
not as another chapter in your healing,
but as a celebration of your aliveness.

Reflection

JOURNAL OR MEDITATION

Prompt:

What would it feel like to stop treating yourself like a project?
What might life open up for you if you trusted your wholeness now?

Gentle Practice:

Do something today with no outcome attached —
no growth, no healing, no deeper meaning.
Just let it be joy.

Whisper:
**"I am not here to be fixed.
I am here to feel free in my life."**

Day Twenty-Six

WANTING SOMETHING DIFFERENT NOW

I was always the 'good' kid.
I got the grades.
Never got into trouble.
I was the student teachers loved —
the daughter parents bragged about.

I followed the rules:
Do well in school.
Go to university.
Get the top grades there too.

And I did.
Not because it always felt good —
but because it felt safe.
When I was responsible, when I was impressive, when I did what was expected...
I was rewarded.
I was seen.
I was protected.

So I stayed on the track —
even when I wasn't sure I liked where it was going.

And I carried that pattern into love.
I stayed too long in a relationship that was never truly right for me.
A relationship that required me to shrink.

To soften my voice.
To quiet my truth.
To become someone more agreeable, easier to love.

I tried to make it work — not because it felt aligned,
but because I was afraid of what it meant to disappoint, to unravel, to choose me.

And somewhere inside that slow and silent unraveling... I forgot who I was.
I looked in the mirror and saw a stranger.
I had followed the rules.
I had done everything "right."
And yet... I felt far from who I really was.

It was a quiet, sacred moment —
the kind that changes everything.
When I realized:
This doesn't fit.
And maybe... it never did.

Soul Speaks

You are allowed to want something different now.
Even if it used to be what you wanted.
Even if it once made sense.
Even if you worked hard to get here.

You are allowed to change.
You are allowed to walk away from a version of you that the world applauded.
You are allowed to outgrow the roles that kept you safe.
You are allowed to say: **this doesn't fit anymore.**

It doesn't mean you were wrong.
It means you're remembering who you are beneath the expectations.

Wanting something new isn't a betrayal.
It's a homecoming.

The *Remembered* Woman

To you, remembered woman...

If you're quietly questioning a life that once felt right —
a job, a dream, a relationship, a belief system...
You are not flaky.
You are not lost.
You are not selfish for pulling back the layers and finding... you.

You are allowed to be dedicated to your growth,
even if it means letting go of the things you once loved.

You are allowed to want something different now.
Even if you're already halfway there.
Even if it means beginning again.
Especially if it means becoming more you.

JOURNAL OR MEDITATION

Prompt:

What part of your life are you holding onto out of loyalty — not alignment?
What would change if you let yourself want something new?

Gentle Practice:

Write down one desire you've been scared to name because it threatens what you've already built.
Then whisper:
"It's safe to evolve.
It's safe to change the story."

Day Twenty-Seven

YOU DON'T HAVE TO BE THE EASY ONE

I used to pride myself on being easy.
Easy to please.
Easy to work with.
Easy to be around.
Easy to love — or so I hoped.

In relationships, I was the one who always said:
"You choose the restaurant."
"Pick the movie."
"Whatever you want — I'm good with it."

I thought I was being flexible.
Chill.
Kind.
The kind of woman who made things simple. Desirable. Low maintenance.

But beneath all that "go with the flow,"
I was craving the foods I actually wanted.
The places that lit up my spirit.
The experiences that felt like me.

And I remember the day I tried to venture out —
I asked my romantic partner if he'd come with me to browse some crystal shops.
It was a small ask — but it mattered.

Not just because I loved it...
But because I wanted to be met where I felt most like myself.

He barely looked up before saying,
"No thanks. I'm going to stay home and play video games."

And just like that, it hit me — the ache of every time I'd deferred.
All the little sacrifices.
All the unchosen meals, the muted desires, the swallowed preferences.
It wasn't just disappointment.
It was an awakening:
I hadn't banked enough "me" moments to balance all I had given away.

Soul Speaks

You are allowed to be someone with needs.
You are allowed to ask.
You are allowed to want.

You do not have to prove your worth by taking up less space.
You do not have to earn love by being low maintenance.
You do not have to starve your soul to stay likable.

Let your needs be known.
Let your desires have a voice.
Let your presence be felt — not edited.

You are allowed to enjoy your favorite foods — the fries, not just the salad.
You are allowed to take the lead.
To say, "This matters to me."
You are allowed to be inconvenient.
You are allowed to be real.
To take up space.
To expect care — and not apologize for it.

Your needs do not make you a burden.
They make you whole.
They make you human.

The *Remembered* Woman

To you, remembered woman...

If you've spent your life making things easier for everyone else,
and silencing your voice just to keep the peace...
Let this be your reminder:

You don't have to be the easy one.
You don't have to be the flexible one.
The accommodating one.
The one who always says "it's fine."

You're allowed to change your mind.
You're allowed to ask for more.
You're allowed to be heard.

You are not too much.
You are simply no longer pretending you don't need anything.
You are not selfish for having preferences.
You are not dramatic for voicing a desire.
You are not less lovable when you speak your truth.

You are remembering what it feels like
to be fully alive in your own life.
Not agreeable.
Not convenient.
Real.

Let yourself want.
Let yourself be met.
Let yourself take up the space you were always worthy of.

JOURNAL OR MEDITATION

Prompt:

Where have you been quieting your needs out of fear you'll be "too much"?
What would it feel like to let those needs have a voice?

Gentle Practice:

Ask for something small today — and let it be received without apology.
Whisper:
**"My needs are sacred.
It is safe to take up space."**

Day Twenty-Eight

BE A LITTLE MESSY

There's a version of me people see on Zoom.
The lighting is good.
The touch-up feature is turned all the way—erasing every pore and every trace of fatigue.
From the shoulders up, I look composed.
Confident.
Like I've got it together.

But Zoom is a perfect metaphor for what so many of us do:
We frame the part that looks good.
We clean the background—or blur it.
We speak clearly, smile politely, and keep the chaos just out of view.

And if the camera panned a little to the left or zoomed out just a bit?
You'd see the trail of Jax's toy cars across the floor—
tiny evidence of big play.
You'd see my favorite sweatpants and mismatched socks—
because who has time to find a matching pair?
(And let's be honest… most of them vanish anyway.)

This is my real life.
Not the one framed for the camera.
Not the one touched-up for display.
But the one that actually exists—loud, imperfect, holy.
And I'm learning to let her be seen.

Because the mess isn't proof I'm failing—
it's proof I'm fully here.

Soul Speaks

You are allowed to be a little messy.
You are allowed to be undone.
You are allowed to not have it all together.

You do not have to earn your belonging through perfection.
You are allowed to take off the polished version of yourself
and show up raw, soft, unsure.

You can miss a deadline.
Let the dishes wait.
Forget to reply.
Need a moment—or a whole day—to come undone.

You are not a brand.
You are a human being.
You are a soul in motion.
A work of art in progress.
A beautiful, sacred mess.

To you, remembered woman...

If you've spent a lifetime keeping it all together—
managing the details, smoothing the edges, adjusting the frame—
so that everything looked okay on the outside...

Let me speak directly to the part of you that's tired.
The part of you that's been performing strength.
The part of you that hides the dishes in the sink before the video call.
The part of you that smiles through exhaustion,
that answers "I'm good!" even when you're anything but.

The *Remembered* Woman

You don't have to keep doing that.
You don't have to be the polished version of yourself just to feel worthy of love or presence.
You don't have to be the one who always holds it all,
while quietly wondering who will hold you.

You are allowed to come as you are.
No filter.
No clean background.
No edited emotion.

Your undone is not unworthy.
Your mess is not a mistake.
Your softness is not a setback.

Let yourself cry if you need to.
Let yourself be seen without explanation.
Let yourself be loved in the version of your life that exists outside the frame.

Because that's the one that's real.
That's the one that matters.
And that's the one your soul came here to live.

You are not too much.
You are simply no longer willing to perform being "fine."
And that is the most beautiful remembering of all.

Reflection

JOURNAL OR MEDITATION

Prompt:

Where in your life are you still pretending to be okay—when what you really want is to be met in your mess?

Gentle Practice:

Do one thing today that feels wonderfully imperfect.
Let something be unfinished.
Let yourself be seen.
Whisper:
**"I am allowed to be messy.
And I am still loved—right here, as I am."**

Day Twenty-Nine

WHEN THE SPEED BECOMES TOO MUCH

I'm really good at moving fast.
I can anticipate what's needed before it's said.
I plan ahead.
I handle what others forget.
I get things done while spinning a dozen plates — and still managing to smile.

For a long time, being quick made me feel powerful.
Quick to solve.
Quick to pivot.
Quick to respond —
to handle, to fix, to move.

And truthfully?
I love speed and efficiency.
If something can be done faster and easier, I'm all for it.
Grocery delivery? Yes, please.
Amazon bringing me garbage bags the second I use the last one?
Brilliant.
It's so much easier than navigating a grocery store with a two-year-old who is passionate about cars —
and whose internal GPS can detect a Hot Wheels display from across the building.

The *Remembered* Woman

Speed has been my superpower.
But somewhere along the way... it became my default.

At one point, I was answering emails while listening to a recorded conference call at 2× speed.
Because anything slower than fast started to feel wrong.
Even my TikTok feed wasn't immune — I had videos playing in fast-forward until my daughter looked at me, confused.
I told her, "They're not talking fast enough."

And the tipping point?
It came in the kitchen.
I was juggling a dozen little tasks while my Stanley was filling from the fridge water dispenser —
grabbing snacks, replying to a message, wiping the counter...
Let's just say the Stanley kept filling.
And filling.

When the sea of water spread across my kitchen floor,
it wasn't just a mess —
it was my soul asking me to slow down.

I'm living life on fast-forward.
And it's too much.
Because being quick all the time doesn't leave space for the magic.
The wonder.
The noticing.

Sometimes the most radical thing I can do is not one more thing — quickly.
Sometimes it's just to stop.
To breathe.
To be in the moment I usually rush past.

Soul Speaks

You are allowed to slow down.
You are allowed to move at the pace of your own breath.
You are allowed to stop chasing and start being.

The world will not fall apart if you take a beat.
The people who love you won't disappear if you pause.
The work will wait.

You don't have to be five steps ahead to be valuable.
You don't have to be in motion to be worthy.

Sometimes your soul wants stillness.
Sometimes your body wants softness.
Sometimes your joy is waiting in the moment you tried to skip.

Let your joy catch up to you.

To you, remembered woman...

Maybe you learned early on that being efficient made you useful.
That being fast made you valuable.
That being the one who "handled it" made you lovable.

So you got really good at doing.
At spinning.
At responding before anyone even had to ask.

You're not broken for becoming that woman.
You were surviving.
You were coping.
You were doing what the world quietly taught you would keep you safe and appreciated.

But beloved, there is more to you than how much you can get done.
You don't have to be quick to be worthy.
You don't have to be endlessly productive to be enough.

The *Remembered* Woman

And if you've been moving so fast that you barely remember the last time you sat without a task—
this is your pause.
This is your invitation to soften.

Not everything needs to be solved right now.
Not every moment needs to be efficient.
You're allowed to just be in it.
Even if the to-do list is still long.
Even if the dishes aren't done.
Even if no one sees how much you're carrying.

You can stop rushing through the miracle of your own life.
You can stop fast-forwarding the parts that are already holy.

Let yourself land inside this breath.
Let your soul feel the stillness.
You don't have to earn your rest.
You just have to remember it's yours.

JOURNAL OR MEDITATION

Prompt:

Where in your life have you been rushing through something that actually deserves to be felt?
What might you notice if you slowed down?

Gentle Practice:

Do something at half-speed today.
Walk slower. Speak slower. Chew slower. Breathe slower.
Whisper:
**"There is no rush.
I can trust the pace of my life."**

Day Thirty

WHAT IF THIS ISN'T IT?

For a long time, I chased the life I thought I was supposed to want —
the achievements.
The house.
The curated milestones that look good in a camera roll.

And to be honest — I actually got a lot of them.
I created the life I had dreamed up years before.
I was even living in a house that looked just like one I aimed to manifest on a walk during my university years.

But even with all of it... something in me was still restless.
Not because I wasn't proud of what I had built —
but because I longed for something deeper.

I wanted more travel.
More adventure.
More sky.
More of the world.

I wanted to explore with my children —
not just routines and packed lunches,
but oceans and spontaneity and shared wonder.

And I also wanted simplicity.
To let go of the performance.
To skip the polished dinner — and go straight to dessert.

To reach more often for what my heart actually desired —
instead of what I thought I was supposed to want.

But that longing felt almost dangerous.
Because I had what I was "supposed" to want.
And yet I couldn't stop asking:
"Is this really it?"

Soul Speaks

You are allowed to want a life that feels good —
not just one that looks good to others.

You are allowed to go off-script.
To change your mind.
To want something softer, slower, deeper, or wilder.

You do not have to perform your happiness.
You are allowed to actually experience it. To live it.

Let your life be shaped by what lights you up —
not what wins applause.

You are allowed to build something that doesn't photograph well,
but feels like freedom in your bones.

To you, remembered woman...

If you've been quietly wondering why the life you built —
the one that looks good on paper —
still feels a little hollow on the inside...
Let me tell you gently:

You're not ungrateful.
You're not lost.
You're not flaky for wanting something more.
You're just remembering yourself.

The *Remembered* Woman

You're just starting to feel the pull toward the version of your life that was always yours —
but maybe didn't fit inside someone else's picture of success.

Maybe you were the girl who followed the rules because you thought it would lead to peace.
Maybe you were the one who checked every box so no one would question your worth.
Maybe you did it all right — and now your soul is asking for something real.

Let this be your invitation to begin again —
not from scratch, but from truth.

You are allowed to reshape your days around what feels good.
You are allowed to start with dessert.
You are allowed to stop performing and start living.

You can still honor the life you built —
while allowing the part of you who's ready to do it differently now.

You can want less — but feel more.
You can want different — and still be on track.
You can rewrite the script — because it's your adventure

Let your life shine like the sun —
not just something to look at,
but a warmth that can be felt from the inside out.

JOURNAL OR MEDITATION

Prompt:

Where have you been chasing a version of life that looks good — but doesn't actually feel aligned?
What would your days look like if they were designed to nourish your soul?

Gentle Practice:

Do one thing today just because it makes you feel good — not because it's impressive, efficient, or expected.
Whisper:
**"I deserve a life that feels like mine.
I'm allowed to begin now."**

Day Thirty-One

BEGIN BEFORE YOU'RE READY

I used to believe there would be a clear sign—
that when the time was right, I'd feel it in my bones.
That I'd feel prepared. Qualified. Confident.
And only then would I begin.

But the sign didn't come.
I went to business school — and somewhere along the way, I learned that everything important had a process.
That there was a right way to build something.
That there were formal steps, clear stages, predictable outcomes.
And if I didn't have those in place… I wasn't ready.

That mindset followed me into my dreams.
I held myself back from starting my business for years —
convinced I needed more time, more structure, more answers.
That I had to do it properly.

It even followed me into travel.
I couldn't book a trip without reading every review, researching every stop, preparing for every possible variable.

But then life gave me something you can't map or research your way through.
I became a mother.
A single mother.

And nothing — not a degree, not a checklist, not a podcast —
can prepare you for that.

There was no "ready."
Just a tiny soul who needed me —
and a version of me that stepped forward.
Ivy needed a mother — and I became her.

And years later I saw it again when Ivy went snorkeling for the first time.
She didn't ease in. She dove.
Just a breath... and the leap.

That's when I knew:
You don't wait for readiness.
You take the plunge — and it meets you there.

Soul Speaks

You are allowed to begin before you feel fully ready.
You are allowed to trust yourself now.
You are allowed to show up — messy, unsure, in your becoming.

There is no moment more sacred than this one.
No version of you more worthy than the one who is still figuring it out.

You don't have to be perfectly healed.
You don't have to be certain.
You don't need a degree in your own destiny.

You don't need certainty. Just a yes — whether it comes as a whisper... or a shout

Begin.
And let it unfold.

The *Remembered* Woman

To you, remembered woman...

If you've been waiting for the perfect moment —
for clarity to arrive,
for confidence to click into place,
for someone to say, "Now is the time" —

Let this be that moment.
Let this be your sign.

Maybe you were taught to wait until you felt sure —
certified, flawless, polished.
But life doesn't work that way.
Becoming doesn't work that way.

You're not behind.
You're not unprepared.
You're just standing at the edge of your own unfolding.

You can begin scared.
You can begin unsure.
You can say yes —
even if your voice shakes,
even if your hands tremble,
even if no one's clapping yet.

You don't need a blueprint.
You just need a seed of trust —
and the courage to dive in.

JOURNAL OR MEDITATION

Prompt:

What are you waiting to feel "ready" for?
What might shift if you gave yourself permission to begin anyway?

Gentle Practice:

Take a small, courageous action toward something you've been putting off.
It doesn't have to be perfect — it just has to be yours.

Whisper:
**"I don't have to wait for perfect.
I begin with me.
I begin now."**

Day Thirty-Two

THE WOMAN YOU USED TO BE

There are versions of me I no longer recognize.
Old beliefs.
Old habits.
Old ways I used to shrink, perform, and bend just to feel wanted.

When I think back to my twenties,
I see a woman who filled her weekends with going out—
drinking, socializing, spending time in loud places
where conversations stayed on the surface.
I didn't always feel like myself in those spaces.
But I kept showing up to them—
because that's what you did when you were single and trying to have fun.
That was the scene. That was the script.

But the kind of connection I truly craved couldn't be found in a dimly lit room
with cheap drinks and louder expectations.
I wanted to be known.
To be loved for who I was — not what I looked like after two cocktails.

And now, when I look back at that version of me,
sometimes I feel the ache of who I used to be.
I sometimes wonder why I stayed in that loop for so long.

The *Remembered* Woman

Why I let myself be judged on a surface I knew held so much depth beneath it.

But here's the thing:
She didn't know better.
And she was trying.
She was figuring out how to belong.
How to be chosen.
How to take up space in a world that never taught her she was enough just as she was.

And she brought me here.

Soul Speaks

You are allowed to outgrow who you used to be.
You are allowed to evolve without guilt.
You are allowed to thank your past self — and still move forward.
You don't have to carry shame just because you've changed.
You are allowed to set down the old armor.
To bless the woman you were.
And to walk freely into who you're becoming.

Growth is not betrayal.
It is the most natural, necessary thing your soul can do.

To you, remembered woman...

Maybe you've been looking back lately.
At the version of you who stayed too long.
Who kept quiet.
Who didn't speak up.
Who let herself be defined by what others saw—
instead of who she knew she was underneath it all.

And maybe part of you still carries guilt.
Guilt for not knowing better.

The *Remembered* Woman

Guilt for the ways you abandoned your own knowing.
Guilt for the spaces you stayed in long after your soul was ready to go.

Let this be your release.
You don't owe your past self an apology.
You owe her compassion.

Because that version of you?
She was doing the best she could with what she knew.
She didn't have the language you have now.
She didn't have the safety.
She didn't have the clarity.

But she still walked.
She still tried.
She still loved with all she had.

And she brought you here.

You are allowed to thank her.
And you are allowed to walk forward without her.

Let this be your whispered goodbye.
Not a goodbye of rejection—
but a goodbye of honor.

She got you this far.
Now you'll carry the rest.
Stronger. Softer.
More whole than ever before.

Reflection

JOURNAL OR MEDITATION

Prompt:

What version of you are you still carrying guilt around—even though she didn't know what you know now? How can you offer her compassion instead?

Gentle Practice:

Write a letter to a former version of yourself.
Let her know she's released. Let her know she did enough.

Whisper:
*"You brought me this far.
Now I'll walk us forward."*

Day Thirty-Three

USING YOUR VOICE ANYWAY

There were so many moments I stayed quiet.
Not because I didn't have something to say —
but because I didn't want to make it awkward.
Didn't want to upset anyone.
Didn't want to seem dramatic, sensitive, or "too much."

And the hardest moments weren't in social circles or family gatherings.
They were in my career.
In an industry still largely dominated by men,
I allowed men to tell me —
directly or indirectly —
that I wasn't capable.
That I didn't belong.
That women couldn't succeed here.

And I said nothing.
I nodded politely.
I swallowed the burn.
I let their words hang in the air without challenge.

And for a long time, I told myself it was easier that way.
That staying quiet was strategic.
That not reacting made me stronger.

But if I'm honest — I wish I had spoken up.
Not just for me.

The *Remembered* Woman

But for the women beside me —
the ones biting their tongues, shrinking their brilliance,
second-guessing their own value in rooms they earned their place in.

And for the women coming up behind me —
the ones with fire in their bellies and sparkle in their eyes,
who would one day be told the same lie I swallowed in silence.

And one day...
for the little girls like my own daughter —
who will walk into this world with brilliance so loud
that it should never have to be quieted
just to be accepted.

Now, I carry my voice like a torch —
not just for me, but for all of us.

Soul Speaks

You are allowed to take up space.
You are allowed to speak when something hurts.
You are allowed to be a full, complex, feeling woman — without apology.

You weren't born to make everyone else feel comfortable.
You do not have to minimize your presence to be lovable.
You do not have to keep shrinking in order to stay safe.

Speak.
Feel.
Shift the energy in the room if it needs to be shifted.
Let your voice be heard — even if it shakes.
Let your truth rise — even if it disrupts the room.

You are allowed to exist unmuted.

The *Remembered* Woman

To you, remembered woman...

If you've been biting your tongue,
playing it cool,
shrinking your soul for the sake of being "easy to be around"...

Let me whisper something you may have forgotten:
You're allowed to speak up.
Even if you've stayed silent for years.
Even if you're afraid of being misunderstood.
Even if no one else in the room is saying what you know in your bones is true.

You don't have to package your passion to make it palatable.
You don't have to water down your truth to keep the peace.

You are allowed to say:
"That hurt me."
"I don't agree."
"This doesn't sit right in my spirit."
"I have something to say."

And you are allowed to take up space while doing it.
Not just the polished, practiced version of you —
but the real one.

The woman who has something to say.
The woman who's been holding it in for far too long.

Let her speak.
Let her take the mic.
Let her be loud.
Let her be free.

Reflection

JOURNAL OR MEDITATION

Prompt:

Where have you been keeping quiet just to keep the peace?
What part of you is ready to be voiced?

Gentle Practice:

Say something today you would normally keep in.
Let it be awkward if it needs to be.

Whisper:
*"I am allowed to take up space.
I will not shrink for anyone.
I am here, whole."*

Day Thirty-Four

WHEN HEALING DOESN'T FEEL LINEAR

I've spent years untangling the knots inside of me.
The patterns, the beliefs, the parts of me that kept choosing what hurt.
I've read the books. Sat with the feelings. Had the hard conversations.
I've reflected. I've grown. I've become more self-aware, more intuitive, more whole.

Especially when it comes to love — and men.
I truly believed I had healed so much.

But then, the pattern shows up again.
I go on a date with someone I already know isn't right.
My body knows — the off-ness, the hesitation,
the quiet red flags waving from the start.

And still, I tell myself:
"Maybe I'm being too quick to judge."
"I should give him a chance."

Even when I've seen this story before.
Even when I know how it ends.

Afterward, I'm not mad at them.
I'm mad at me — for ignoring what I already knew.
For ignoring my own knowing.
For stepping into the same kind of dynamic I swore I had outgrown.

And then the voice creeps in:
"Why am I still attracting this?"
"Haven't I healed this already?"
"Am I doing something wrong?"

But I'm learning...
Healing doesn't mean I never slip into old patterns.
It means I see them sooner.
It means I leave faster.
It means I love myself enough to stop the cycle.
Even when it stings.

Soul Speaks

You are allowed to still be healing and have rough days.
You are allowed to feel the progress and the tension.

You don't have to prove your growth by being perfectly calm.

Healing isn't a finish line.
It's a deepening.
A remembering.
A softening.

It's the choice to return to yourself,

again and again, in acceptance and love—
even after the storm.

To you, remembered woman...

If you've been showing up for yourself —
doing the work, feeling the feelings, unlearning the patterns,
and you still catch yourself in an old story...

Maybe a relationship you knew wasn't aligned.
Or a dynamic that looked different on the outside but felt too familiar

The *Remembered* Woman

on the inside.
Or a yes that didn't feel good in your body, but you said it anyway…

Let me tell you something your soul already knows:
This is still healing.
This is not failure.
This is not proof that you're broken.
This is not a setback.
This is a checkpoint.
A sacred one.

Because this time — you noticed.
This time — you heard the whisper.
This time — maybe you left sooner.
Maybe you forgave faster.
Maybe you remembered yourself even while you were in it.

That is progress.
You don't have to fake perfection to prove you're evolving.

You are allowed to be wise and messy.
Soft and reactive.
Healing and human.

And you are allowed to try again.
Not from scratch — but from compassion.

And wisdom.

Reflection

JOURNAL OR MEDITATION

Prompt:

Where are you still holding yourself to a standard of perfection — even as you're in the middle of your healing?
What would it feel like to soften and release that pressure?

Gentle Practice:

When you catch yourself repeating a pattern,
pause and place a hand on your heart.
Say to yourself:
*"This, too, is part of my healing.
I return to myself now.
I am still safe here."*

Day Thirty-Five

LET IT BE EASY

I was raised by a single mother —
a woman who, at one point, worked five jobs at once.
If that wasn't the definition of hard work, I didn't know what was.

That became the standard.
The silent message:
If you want something, you hustle for it.
You earn it.
You sacrifice for it.

So when I started my business, I did what I was taught.
I studied the sales books.
I followed the training.
I learned the strategies, the scripts, the follow-up sequences.
There were timelines, touchpoints, trackers.

It was constant output. Constant effort.

And then, something shifted.
The strategy didn't change — I did.

I started showing up from a place of purpose.
I shared my why.
Why I cared about this work.
Why it mattered.
Why I believed in it — and in the people I was serving.

And that changed everything.

The *Remembered* Woman

Clients started reaching out.
Opportunities flowed in.
The "chase" disappeared.
No push.

Just alignment.
Just truth.

I felt it again in my healing journey.
I used to believe the only way through trauma was years of heavy lifting.
But then I tried something simple —
a meditation, a reimagining, a new ending to an old pain.

I let myself rewrite the story gently.
And something deep inside me shifted.

The ache loosened.
The weight lifted.

And just like that...
it worked.

It was easy — and it was real.

And I realized:
Hard isn't always more noble.
And ease isn't a shortcut.
Sometimes it's a sign you're finally aligned.

Soul Speaks

You are allowed to choose ease.
You are allowed to follow what flows.
You are allowed to trust what feels gentle — not just what feels hard.

Everything doesn't have to be a proving ground.
You don't have to suffer for your worth.
You don't have to grit your way to the good things.

The *Remembered* Woman

> Let things be soft if they want to be.
> Let things be simple if they show up that way.
> Let your joy be easy.
> Let your healing be gentle.
>
> You don't have to fight to be free.

To you, remembered woman...

If you've always taken the uphill path —
if you've been taught that pain makes it more meaningful,
that the harder you work, the more deserving you become…

Let this be your quiet permission:
You're allowed to let it be easy now.

You don't have to prove your worth through burnout.
You don't have to climb your way into receiving.
You don't have to break down before something good finds you.

What if it's allowed to flow?
What if it's allowed to arrive without struggle?
What if softness is not a sign of weakness — but of healing?

Ease doesn't mean you're not doing enough.
Ease means you're listening.
It means you're aligned.
It means you're finally not resisting the very thing your soul has been asking for:
A life that feels like yours — with no prerequisite for struggle or hard work.

Reflection

JOURNAL OR MEDITATION

Prompt:

Where in your life are you choosing "hard" out of habit — even when ease is available?
What would it look like to let it be easier?

Gentle Practice:

Today, follow the path of least resistance.
Say yes to the thing that flows.
Let the simple choice be the sacred one.

Whisper:
"I can let it be easy."

Day Thirty-Six

THE ACHE OF LETTING GO

There's a strange ache that comes with growth.
Not just because of how much you've stretched—
but because of what you've had to leave behind.

For me, it was friendships.
In my school years and well into my twenties,
I prioritized them above almost everything.

Some of those relationships lasted decades—
they were part of my foundation, my identity, my normal.

But as I changed, something shifted.
I started to realize that the people who had known me for years…
didn't really know me anymore.
They knew the older version—
the one who adapted, who blended in,
who never made things uncomfortable.

But not the woman I was becoming.

At first, I tried to hold on.
To pretend it still fit.
To maintain the connection, even if it felt hollow.

Because who wants to walk away from history?
From comfort? From belonging?

The *Remembered* Woman

But eventually, I had to be honest with myself:
**Belonging isn't about who's known you the longest.
It's about who sees you now.**

Letting go wasn't easy.
But it was necessary.

And what I feared would feel like emptiness
slowly began to feel like space.

Soul Speaks

You are allowed to let go of what no longer fits.
You are allowed to release what once served you—but doesn't anymore.
You are allowed to create space.

You are not obligated to stay in a version of life that no longer feels like yours.
You are not required to hold on just because it's familiar.

You are allowed to change your mind.
To end the chapter.
To shed the identity.
To release the role.

Grief may come—and it's allowed too.
But don't mistake grief for misalignment.

You are allowed to let go with grace.

The *Remembered* Woman

To you, remembered woman...

Maybe something in you has been tugging—
a quiet knowing that a certain connection, rhythm, role, or title
just doesn't feel like home anymore.

Maybe you've tried to make it fit.
Tried to keep showing up.
Tried to tell yourself it's just a phase.

But there's another truth stirring too—
one you've been hearing in your bones:

It's okay to outgrow what once felt right.

It doesn't mean you're ungrateful.
It doesn't mean you're abandoning anyone.
It means you are honoring who you are now.

You don't have to keep shrinking.

You don't have to keep pretending for the sake of shared history.

You're allowed to be the one who leaves—
not out of anger,
but because your soul is ready to breathe deeper.

Letting go might feel like loss at first.
But space is not emptiness.
It's an invitation.
And you're allowed to answer it.

JOURNAL OR MEDITATION

Prompt:

What are you still holding onto—not because it fits, but because you're afraid of the space it might leave? What would it feel like to trust the letting go?

Gentle Practice

Release one small thing today that no longer reflects the woman you're becoming.
It could be an object, a routine, a plan, or even a role.
Let it be a sacred release.

Whisper:
*"Letting go isn't failure.
It's freedom."*

Day Thirty-Seven

THE WOMAN YOU WERE ALWAYS MEANT TO BE

I turned forty and thought I should have a list.
You know — the big one.
Goals to chase. Things to accomplish.
Milestones to hit before the next decade.

But when I sat down to write it,
I realized I didn't want a list.
I didn't want more pressure.
I didn't want more work.

I wanted space.
I wanted to just be.

And something surprising happened when I gave myself that—
Life still moved.
Things still happened.
But they didn't feel forced.
They flowed.

I thought of our trip to Hawaii—
the days where nothing was planned,
and yet they ended up being the most magical.

Chasing waves with Jax.
Getting caught in the rain with Ivy.

The *Remembered* Woman

Eating shaved ice for dinner and laughing so hard we could barely breathe.

We didn't need an itinerary.
We just needed each other.
And presence.

That's when I knew—
I didn't have to push anymore to make something meaningful.
My life was already full of meaning.

And I didn't need to become someone else to finally feel at home.
I was already her.
The woman I was always meant to be.

Soul Speaks

You are allowed to be the woman you came here to be.
You are allowed to take up space, rewrite the story,
and rise as someone your past never saw coming.

You are not too much.
You are not behind.
You are not broken.

You are becoming.
You are remembering.
You are rising.

And the world is ready for the woman you've fought so hard to meet.

To you, remembered woman...

This book began with a conversation—
a soul speaking to her own reflection.

And maybe, along the way,
you started to hear something too.

The *Remembered* Woman

Maybe you began to remember—
that your voice matters.
That your story is sacred.
That your desires are not accidents.

Maybe you started to believe—
that the most radical thing you could do
is stop performing... and just be you.

So let this final message be an invitation—
not to fix, not to strive... but to remember and return.

To your softness.
To your truth.
To your power.
To your name.

To you, remembered woman...

You were already the chosen one.
The first picked.
The one your soul entrusted with this life,
this path,
this remembering.

You've always been her.
Now... you're just ready to live like it.

JOURNAL OR MEDITATION

Prompt:

What part of yourself are you ready to reclaim?
What truth have you finally remembered?

Gentle Practice

Write a note from your future self—
the one who has fully stepped into her power.
Ask her: *What do you want me to know right now?*

Whisper:
*"I remember who I am.
And I'm ready to live like it."*

A Final Gift

YOU WILL NOT FORGET

To you, remembered woman—

Now that you've remembered…
you will not forget.

Not in the same way.

You may still have moments of doubt.
Moments when the old voices grow loud again.
Moments when the world tries to convince you to shrink.

But something has awakened now.
And that knowing—your knowing—cannot be undone.

You've seen yourself clearly.
You've heard the voice beneath the noise.
You've touched the truth of who you are.

And once a woman remembers,
she can't go back to pretending.

So when the world tries to pull you back into the roles,
the masks,
the hustle,
the silence…

The *Remembered* Woman

Pause.
Breathe.
And whisper:

**"I remember who I am.
And I will not forget again."**

This is your gift.
This is your becoming.
This is your return.

And it is forever.

ACKNOWLEDGEMENTS

To the women who have shared their stories with me, held me in my own remembering, and reminded me of what is possible when we live from soul—thank you.

To my children, for being the greatest mirrors and teachers of all.

And to every remembered woman reading this— Thank you for being here. Thank you for choosing to remember.

ABOUT THE AUTHOR

Kalee Boisvert is a writer, speaker, mother, and guide for women who are ready to remember who they really are. Her writing invites women to awaken to truth, reclaim their power, and create lives that are aligned, honest, and deeply free.

www.ingramcontent.com/pod-product-compliance
Lightning Source LLC
Chambersburg PA
CBHW050328010526
44119CB00050B/718